The Power of 1°

Leader's Guide

Essential One-Year Devotional Series for Worship Ministries

MARK MATTINGLY

To make the most of these devotionals, have your team members use the companion book:

"The Power of 1° - Participant's Guide"

Acknowledgments

"The Power of 1°" was birthed from a culmination of truths about God, scripture and life that have been poured into me by more people than I can possibly acknowledge. From pastors, mentors, Bible Study leaders, Sunday School teachers, family, friends, colleagues and more, they have all impacted this book in more ways than I can imagine.

With this in mind, there are some very special people I would like to thank. First, I want to thank my wife, Tonya. I don't know how to even begin thanking you for your seemingly never-ending love, support and patience with me. I love you. For our four sons: Tyler, Blake, Hudson and Jack. For helping me laugh more than I deserve and love deeper than I thought possible. It is a blessing to be a father to such incredible young men. For my parents raising me in a Godly home. Thanks to my great graphics artist, James Tyree. Also, for all of the family members, friends, editors and others that contributed to this book coming to fruition. Most importantly, I want to thank my Lord for being my Hope, my Salvation and my God. You are everything to me.

Dedication

To my beautiful wife, Tonya,
and our four sons: Tyler, Blake, Hudson and Jack

Shaded Edition: The words of Jesus Christ
can be found *shaded* throughout the scripture verses.

First Printing 2017
Printed in the United States of America

Cover Design: James Tyree

ISBN 978-0-9990080-0-3

For more information, contact us at:
PowerOfOneDegree@gmail.com

Table of Contents

True Story

Years ago, an eight-year-old boy attended an evening worship service at a church in the Midwest. While voices sang and instruments played, God began to speak to the young lad. As the service ended and the family headed home, the young boy was heavy-hearted. From the back seat of the car, the son leaned forward and whispered to his dad that he needed to talk with him. When they got home, the son told his father he felt God was speaking to him. There was something he was supposed to do, but the son didn't quite understand it all. The father went with the son to his room and shared the Good News of the Gospel with him. The son prayed to accept Jesus Christ as his Lord and Savior on the edge of his bed that night.

Do you know who the son was? That was me. An average little boy in a typical, Midwestern church surrendered his life to Jesus through a seemingly ordinary worship service. The people leading worship that evening were unaware that God had used them to point me to Christ. Through their service and obedience, my life was changed forever. What the worship leader did that night impacted me for eternity. Likewise, what you do each and every week as a worship leader can also be used by God to impact souls for eternity.

Be encouraged: What you do as a worship leader each week matters. You never know what extraordinary activities God is doing in what appears to be an ordinary worship service. Be faithful in pointing people to Christ in every worship service you lead. Be prayed up and expect God to do amazing things each week. Only He can do the extraordinary with the ordinary...

Introduction

As a worship leader, you pour your heart into creating the best worship experience possible. You are responsible for a countless number of activities such as music selection, orders of worship and rehearsals. While these are all necessary activities for a successful worship experience, there may be an essential element that's missing: a weekly spiritual growth time with your worship ministry team. Is your team growing deeper together in their spiritual walk? Are you leading them through a dynamic devotional each week that is intended to help worship teams grow in their relationship with Christ? This is what *"The Power of 1°"* is specifically designed to do.

"The Power of 1°" seeks to align worship leaders and team members with what God intended worship to be about: *Him*. To become better leaders of worship, it is imperative we get to know God, the object of our worship, better. By using "The Power of 1°" over the next 52 weeks, you and your team will embark on an adventure to learn more about God and worship. Your team will be challenged through these five-minute weekly devotionals to see worship from God's perspective and align their hearts with His. *"The Power of 1°, Leader's Guide"* will help you lead your team while each team member can follow along in their own *"The Power of 1°, Participant's Guide"*.

I trust you will grow deeper in love with Jesus, more clearly understand your role as a worship leader and become more effective in leading others into the presence of God. It is my privilege to join you as you travel the road of this new spiritual journey. It is my prayer that these devotionals will help propel you and your team closer to Him.

Mark Mattingly

Note: *The worship leader should use "The Power of 1° - Leader's Guide" to lead the team while worship ministry team members follow along in "The Power of 1° - Participant's Guide".* Also, while these devotionals can be used in a variety of ways, we encourage you to consider using them as a five-minute devotional accompanying your weekly worship practices. Throughout this book you will find references to "worship ministries". For the purpose of this book, these references are synonymous with other titles, such as worship teams, praise teams, choirs, bands, orchestras and similar groups. Regardless of how your church worship structure is set up, I trust this book will help elevate you to new heights in your worship and relationship with God.

[Optional Materials: A globe or spherical object]

Proverbs 4:27
27 *Do not swerve to the right or to the left; turn your foot away from evil.*

God is telling us in this passage to keep our eyes and heart laser-focused on the ultimate target, which is Christ. It says we are to run from evil – to flee from it rather than fighting it in our own strength. We are to maintain a direct path to our Lord and not deviate either to the right or to the left. In other words, our lives should be obsessively fixated on Him and being in the absolute center of His will.

Satan opposes this focused perspective. He knows that God's followers will not choose to run 180° in the opposite direction from their Lord. So he begins with the smallest spiritual cracks and continually works to widen them into chasms between us and God. It may start with a jealous thought here. A prideful feeling there. A lustful thought one day. A judgmental statement the next. Before we know it, God taps us on our spiritual shoulders and asks why we are so far from Him. The smallest acts of disobedience can grow into our greatest barriers to authentic worship.

Think of it this way - If you took a trip following the equator all the way around the earth, you would travel 24,901 miles to get back to your original location. But if you began at the same starting place and travelled around the world, being only one degree off course the entire time, you would end up 434 miles away from your original starting point! That is wider than the entire state of Kansas or over 7,600 football fields in distance! If we are not attune to God's voice, only 1° off course can lead us a long way away from our intended destination – Christ.

But worshipper, be encouraged: the inverse is true as well! Every step we take toward Christ has an enormous impact on our spiritual life. We need to follow the wisdom of this verse and realize that pursuing God and His will is the ultimate goal. We need to be steadfast and vigilant in pursuing Christ at all times. Not His blessings. Not even answered prayers. But Christ Himself.

Are you vigilant in your pursuit of your Lord? Is your worship focused on Him and nothing else? Be alert and attentive to His voice so you can remain focused on Him and be in the center of His will.

Question(s) of the Week: *Are you seeking God and His will for your life, or your own?*

Worship Leader: *Ask your team: What are some common distractions we face as we follow Christ and His direction for our lives?*

_____ **The Power of 1°**

Nehemiah 3:1

1 Then Eliashib the high priest rose up with his brothers the priests, and they built the Sheep Gate. They consecrated it and set its doors. They consecrated it as far as the Tower of the Hundred, as far as the Tower of Hananel.

Nehemiah was arguably one of the greatest leaders of the Old Testament. Just a little history here... In chapter one, Nehemiah was informed that his home city, Jerusalem, was in shambles and the Jews who escaped were in great trouble. Nehemiah cried out to God for favor and for the restoration of Jerusalem. In chapter two, heavy-hearted Nehemiah approached King Artaxerxes and asked permission to rebuild the city of Jerusalem. After receiving both permission and letters for safe travel from the king, Nehemiah left on his journey.

Nehemiah took army officers and horsemen with him but did not share with them what God had laid on his heart. Going by himself during the cover of night, Nehemiah assessed the area, counted the cost and gathered the people necessary to rebuild Jerusalem. Jerusalem was a very important city, so building strong walls and defenses was essential. Eliashib, the high priest, joined other priests in rebuilding Jerusalem. Why would the priests build it? Why not carpenters or ironsmiths?

Surely there were more qualified builders around than the priests.

The priests began with building the Sheep Gate. Why did they build the Sheep Gate first? Why didn't they build a tower, such as the Tower of Hananel or Tower of the Hundred as a lookout? Or what about building the Broad Wall first? It was the strongest portion and greatest defense throughout Jerusalem. Or maybe a different gate, such as the Horse Gate, Valley Gate or Fountain Gate. Why the Sheep Gate? What was so important about it?

Here is the answer: The Sheep Gate was used to bring sheep into the city to be sacrificed in the temple as an offering to God. The Sheep Gate was built first, to show the priority and importance of worship! Nehemiah and his people worshipped God before they did anything else. And the priests were God's chosen people to build the gate and sanctify it. Nehemiah understood it was God he was ultimately serving. He set an incredible example for us to follow in establishing worship to God as our number one priority. Are you following his lead?

Question(s) of the Week: Is knowing God and worshipping Him your top priority?

Worship Leader: Challenge your team: Evaluate your life to see if there is anything that has taken priority over the Lord.

James 4:6

6 *But he gives more grace. Therefore it says, "God opposes the proud, but gives grace to the humble."*

Pride is defined as *inordinate self-esteem or conceit.* Pride is one of the deadliest sins we commit because it manifests itself within so many other sins. For example, when we are selfish, pride says we deserve something more than someone else. Pride tells us we shouldn't have to apologize to others. It says we are better than the people around us. Pride causes us to think we are above menial tasks within our worship ministry. It keeps us from respecting others by showing up late for rehearsals. Pride says we are too good to practice with everyone else.

In contrast, humility is the opposite of pride. Humility is exercised when we lower ourselves in relation to other people. This is against our human nature and hard to do sometimes, isn't it? We tend to believe people will take advantage of us. We may become their doormat. They may walk all over us. While sometimes this may be the case, God specifically tells us in this verse that He opposes the proud. Think about it... Do you really want to be in opposition to God? You are, if you are living a life of pride. Conversely, when you live your life with humility, He adorns you with grace. Sounds like a much better relationship, doesn't it?

Pride may be the most prevalent sin found in worship ministries today. Guitarists and pianists struggle with it. Sopranos and sound techs are vulnerable to its grasp. In fact, every instrumentalist and vocalist faces this temptation. The reality is that none of us chose our musical gifts. They were given to each of us by God, exclusively for His glory. We are no better than others who do not have the musical talents we have been blessed with.

As God's musicians, why do we *take possession* of the musical gifts He has entrusted to us? It is all from Him, for Him. He gifted us with the musical abilities we have so we can participate in bringing Him glory. Praise Him for the musical talents you have, but be careful not to become prideful with them.

Question(s) of the Week: *Have the skills and talents God has entrusted to you turned into pride or arrogance in any way?*

Worship Leader: *Pray now: Ask God to keep you and your worship ministry team members humble regarding the musical gifts and talents they have been blessed with.*

———————————————————————— *The Power of 1°*

Matthew 18:15-17

15 "If your brother sins against you, go and tell him his fault, between you and him alone. If he listens to you, you have gained your brother.

16 But if he does not listen, take one or two others along with you, that every charge may be established by the evidence of two or three witnesses.

17 If he refuses to listen to them, tell it to the church. And if he refuses to listen even to the church, let him be to you as a Gentile and a tax collector."

Misunderstandings, disagreements and conflicts will happen. How we respond to them determines if we are mature believers or not. Conflict creates division and can fester into bitterness, resentment and unforgiveness. This is exactly what Satan wants – to divide and attack us as Christians and destroy our ability to effectively serve God.

We cannot truly worship God as long as there is conflict and dissention between us and other people. This conflict may be with church leaders, church members or even within our worship ministry. We each need to be honest and personally evaluate if there is even a hint of dissention that we need to address.

God's prescription for how we handle conflicts between Christians is clearly found in these verses. Notice it doesn't say to talk with several others first. He has laid out a precise process of how we are to go about mending relationships with other believers. The ultimate objective here is to restore a Godly relationship between the specific people involved.

If we are honest, sometimes we struggle with starting the conversation. We may use excuses like *"they're the one that offended me – they should initiate and apologize"*! But scripture clearly states that we are the ones to initiate the conversation - not the person that committed the offense. Why? Because it is our relationship with God and the offender that is suffering the most. Additionally, the one that committed the offense may not even be aware of the offense or depth of it. To get back into a right relationship with them and God, we are to be the ones to initiate the conversation.

Sometimes our pride gets in the way of us resolving the conflict. We may even avoid people completely just so we don't have to deal with the situation. Neither of these actions are how God desires for us to resolve conflicts. It can be hard to address them, but by doing so, we are being obedient to God. It will also free us to more authentically worship Him by dealing with these issues rather than ignoring them.

Question(s) of the Week: *Is there <u>any</u> believer you currently have an unresolved conflict with? What steps will you take to resolve the situation and get into a right relationship with both them and God?*

Worship Leader: *Encourage your team: If you have any unresolved conflict with others, please address it ASAP.*

―――――――――――――――――――――――――――――― **The Power of 1°**

Matthew 5:43-47

43 *"You have heard that it was said, 'You shall love your neighbor and hate your enemy.'*

44 *But I say to you, Love your enemies and pray for those who persecute you,*

45 *so that you may be sons of your Father who is in heaven. For he makes his sun rise on the evil and on the good, and sends rain on the just and on the unjust.*

46 *For if you love those who love you, what reward do you have? Do not even the tax collectors do the same?*

47 *And if you greet only your brothers, what more are you doing than others? Do not even the Gentiles do the same?"*

In this passage, Jesus is explaining the difference between the incorrect traditions of the religious rulers and the teachings of Jesus. The Jewish leaders of His day were inaccurately teaching that *neighbors* were only those people they chose to call their friends. If someone was not their friend, they were considered an enemy and were not classified as their *neighbors*. The Jewish rulers were trying to narrow the law, making it easier to obey. Jesus was widening their view of the definition to include all people, correcting their improper teaching and revealing their hidden sin.

Jesus gives us two commands here. The first is to love our enemies. Loving our enemies is not the same as avoiding them. It is choosing to have a proactive, interactive relationship of blessing others. Anyone can love their friends – that's easy. Non-believers do this quite well and more often than we would care to admit, better than Christians! But loving our enemies is much more difficult. This is something non-believers cannot fully do. Only Christians are able to truly do this because the Holy Spirit empowers and enables us to love our enemies through His divine power.

The second point is to pray for those who persecute us. Jesus gives us a beautiful picture of this when He was on the cross and said *Father, forgive them, for they know not what they do.* (Luke 23:34a). This was stated by Jesus out of a pure love for those who put Him on the cross. Like Jesus, we should forgive those who persecute us. Harboring unforgiveness creates division between us and others, affecting our ability to authentically worship Him.

Be honest with yourself: Is there anyone within our church or worship ministry that you struggle to love? Do you sincerely desire for your "*enemies*", or those people you don't get along with, to be blessed? Do you pray for their salvation and relationship with Christ if they are lost? Have you forgiven them or are you harboring resentment and bitterness toward them? Ask God to reveal these people to you right now and pray God will help you to love them.

Question(s) of the Week: *Who is God bringing to your mind that you need to love and/or forgive?*

Worship Leader: *Encourage your worship ministry members to ask God for the ability to love those around them that are difficult to love.*

———————————————————— **The Power of 1°**

1 John 2:3

3 *And by this we know that we have come to know him, if we keep his commandments.*

This scripture gives us the formula for confirming we know Christ. Obedience is a telltale sign of Christ existing in our lives. A child that obeys their parents indicates there is a healthy respect for authority. When we obey our bosses, teachers and other leaders, it reveals we are submissive to those in authority over us. In Christianity, obeying God's commands means so much more. Obeying God is indicative of the life change that only comes through Christ. If a person says they are a Christian but there is little or no evidence of a changed life, it is fair to question whether they are a true believer at all.

When John wrote in this verse that we should keep God's commandments, it doesn't mean we choose to obey some and not others. Our effort and desire goes into obeying all of them. This doesn't mean we will never sin or that we are above being tempted. Even Jesus was tempted by Satan (Matthew 4:1-11). But it does indicate we can withstand temptation just as Jesus did, with the help of the Holy Spirit.

Doing good things alone does not produce a personal relationship with Christ. For example, it is possible for you to be part of our worship ministry, sing and play music and still not know Christ. It is possible, but it cannot be worship. True worship can only be offered by a true believer. But a personal relationship with Christ does produce Godly works. This is demonstrated by obedience to God's commands as this verse states.

Do you claim to be a believer but there is little or no evidence to back it up? Maybe you are new to our worship ministry. Maybe you have been involved for many years. If you don't know for sure you are a true believer, do some soul-searching. You need to be absolutely certain God claims you as His own. Your eternity is in the balance.

Obedience is the measuring stick by which we validate God's presence in our lives. How do you measure up? Do you know God's commandments and are you obeying them? Now is the time to make sure you really know Him.

Question(s) of the Week: *Would Christians close to you say there is significant evidence to indicate you are a believer? Why or why not?*

Worship Leader: *Challenge your team: Take a minute now to seriously assess and evaluate your level of obedience to God and His Word.*

─────────────────────────────── *The Power of 1°*

[Optional Materials: A metal or PVC pipe **]**

Deuteronomy 5:7

7 *You shall have no other gods before me.*

God makes it very clear in both Deuteronomy 5:7 and Exodus 20:3 that we are to put God above everything else. There is no question what the scriptures mean and no reasonable way to *misinterpret* this clear and concise command. Even in our best efforts, though, Satan wants to distract and deceive us. Satan knows the best counterfeit to authentically worshipping God is worshipping the closest thing to God. He is cunning. He is deceptive. He understands our weaknesses.

This pipe may not seem like much, but it represents one of the greatest idols prevalent in churches today. We call this a pipe, but it more accurately could be referred to as a *conduit*. A conduit carries an object from one place to another. Worship, or music, is a conduit. It can be used to take us from our everyday lives to the throne room of God.

Unfortunately, many people in churches today worship the *conduit of worship* rather than worshipping God. This is seen when we put great value on *our* preferences, *our* musical likes and dislikes and *our* desired style of worship. Our attention becomes misguided when we focus on the music rather than on Christ. We become distracted from bringing praise to God by looking at *our* own desires rather than His.

True worship transcends the conduit's makeup – it goes beyond a style of music. It is deeper than the age of a song. It takes us further than our preferences of the lyrics. God-honoring, authentic worship occurs any time we are able to focus our heart and attention only on God. He should be the one and only object of our worship. Anything less than directly worshipping Him is a far distant second in quality and is not pleasing to God.

As we grow in our faith, our worship shifts from our own personal preferences to God becoming the only object of our worship. If we are still wrestling with anything that is not directly focused on bringing our praise and worship before God, we have settled for counterfeit worship. It is time for us to grow beyond *our* preferences, *our* styles and *our* desires and instead, worship God and God alone.

Question(s) of the Week: *How are you currently "worshipping the conduit" of worship, rather than worshipping God?*

Worship Leader: *Ask your team: What other "idols" do we sometimes unintentionally worship instead of God? (i.e. Prayer? Devotion to God? Good works?)*

The Power of 1°

Genesis 4:1-7

1 Now Adam knew Eve his wife, and she conceived and bore Cain, saying, "I have gotten a man with the help of the LORD."

2 And again, she bore his brother Abel. Now Abel was a keeper of sheep, and Cain a worker of the ground.

3 In the course of time Cain brought to the LORD an offering of the fruit of the ground,

4 and Abel also brought of the firstborn of his flock and of their fat portions. And the LORD had regard for Abel and his offering,

5 but for Cain and his offering he had no regard. So Cain was very angry, and his face fell.

6 The LORD said to Cain, "Why are you angry, and why has your face fallen?

7 If you do well, will you not be accepted? And if you do not do well, sin is crouching at the door. Its desire is contrary to you, but you must rule over it."

Both Cain and Abel brought offerings to God. They each sacrificed from what they worked at – Cain brought fruit from his field and Abel offered up the *firstborn* from his flock – the best of all he had. Both occupations were considered admirable. Both brothers knew what was required of them and the sacrifices God expected. But only one brother's sacrifice was accepted by God. It says God *"had regard"*, or accepted Abel's sacrifice but not Cain's.

Did God show favoritism here? Is it that God desires meat sacrifices over fruit? Does God prefer to accept the younger brother as the underdog? Was it the sacrifice that caused God to approve of Abel's but not Cain's, or is there more to the story than this?

If we look deeper, we understand that it was Abel's *faith* that caused his sacrifice to be acceptable to God. Cain presented his sacrifice out of disbelief, not out of faith (Heb. 11:4). God's acceptance of one gift over the other was less about the sacrifice itself and more about the heart in which it was given. Abel presented his sacrifice of worship out of obedience, in response to what was in God's best interest and desire. Cain presented his sacrifice from what he personally desired rather than obedience to God.

When Cain realized his sacrifice was unacceptable to God, he became angry rather than repentant. His pride kept him from seeing his sin. He was focused on himself rather than God. God stated Cain's sacrifice would be accepted if it was done out of faith and obedience but this was not the manner in which Cain responded.

We are called to bring a sacrifice of worship and praise to God. This is to be done out of faith rather than obligation – from our hearts rather than merely in our actions. Hebrews 11:6 tells us that *"without faith it is impossible to please God"*.

Is your worship driven by your faith in Christ? Faith is the means by which we have a right relationship with Him and the only way our worship is accepted by Him.

Question(s) of the Week: *Is your personal worship led by faith or out of obligation each week?*

Worship Leader: *Ask your team: What are some areas where a person's worship may not be God-honoring and how can it be corrected?*

————————————————————————— *The Power of 1°*

Numbers 12:1-10a

1 Miriam and Aaron spoke against Moses because of the Cushite woman whom he had married, for he had married a Cushite woman.

2 And they said, "Has the Lord indeed spoken only through Moses? Has he not spoken through us also?" And the Lord heard it.

3 Now the man Moses was very meek, more than all people who were on the face of the earth.

4 And suddenly the Lord said to Moses and to Aaron and Miriam, "Come out, you three, to the tent of meeting." And the three of them came out.

5 And the Lord came down in a pillar of cloud and stood at the entrance of the tent and called Aaron and Miriam, and they both came forward.

6 And he said, "Hear my words: If there is a prophet among you, I the Lord make myself known to him in a vision; I speak with him in a dream.

7 Not so with my servant Moses. He is faithful in all my house.

8 With him I speak mouth to mouth, clearly, and not in riddles, and he beholds the form of the Lord. Why then were you not afraid to speak against my servant Moses?"

9 And the anger of the Lord was kindled against them, and he departed.

10a When the cloud removed from over the tent, behold, Miriam was leprous, like snow.

Even the greatest families have challenges! How many of you have brothers or sisters? This is a great story involving family dynamics. Sometimes it is comforting to know that every family has their difficulties!

Moses' own brother and sister, Aaron and Miriam, called Moses out on two items: Miriam and Aaron were upset because of Moses' marriage to a Cushite woman and the power she carried. More importantly, they were questioning if God spoke with Moses differently and more exclusively than He did with them.

The Lord makes it clear that He has a special relationship with Moses. Unlike other prophets where He makes Himself known through a vision or dream, the Lord speaks to Moses face to face. In fact, God spoke to Moses in broad daylight and through normal conversations. Most likely Miriam began this quarrel, indicated by her name being mentioned first. Also, because of Miriam's lack of honor and respect towards God's servant and messenger Moses, she was plagued with leprosy.

Moses was known for many things, such as the burning bush, the Ten Commandments, leading the Israelites out of Egypt and stuttering when he talked. But he was also known for something else: Moses' meekness and humility. In fact, many times Moses would defend God's character, such as when the golden calf was made by the Israelites while he went up Mount Sinai to get the Ten Commandments. But here, Moses' personal character is being called into question yet he doesn't defend it. He allows God to take up his defense rather than himself.

Unfortunately humility is not a characteristic mentioned much these days in relation to worship leaders and worship team members. In fact, often it is quite the opposite. Pride and arrogance seem to be more prevalent in today's worship ministries, as if somehow we are above others.

In reality, we should lead in our humility. According to James 4:10, we are called to *humble ourselves before the Lord* and as leaders in the worship of God, the meekness and humility should begin with us. Let's humble ourselves before God and make little of us, so we can make much of Him.

Question(s) of the Week: *Would your closest friends describe you as "humble"? If not, what evidence is there that gives them this impression?*

Worship Leader: *Pray now: Pray that God will help you and your team to be humble before Him and that He removes any pride within the team.*

The Power of 1°

Role Models

[**Optional Materials:** Picture of a popular role model]

Ephesians 5:1

1 Therefore be imitators of God, as beloved children.

Think about your life for a moment... Who are you a big *fan* of? Is it a sports figure, a movie star, a Christian artist or maybe an author? Why are you intrigued by them and drawn to them? And what evidence do you have that indicates you're a fan?

We all tend to follow our role models. We read about them. We may talk like them. Sing like them. Act like them. Play like them. Study their stats. We even own books, CD's, DVD's, jerseys, hats, and other paraphernalia that represent and symbolize them. We examine what makes them unique and special.

While it is human nature to follow our role models, our focus should change as we grow in our relationship with Christ. As sanctification occurs in our lives, the world begins to dim and our Lord shines through. The definition of who our role model is shifts from where it has been to a new direction. Our attention and affection turns to a new audience – an audience of One – Jesus Christ.

Paul is encouraging us here in Ephesians to imitate Christ. According to scholars, this is the only place in scripture where the word *imitate* refers to our relationship as Christians with our Heavenly Father. As worshippers of Almighty God, having Jesus as our role model should trump all other role models. There shouldn't even be a close second. He stands alone. There is no scale that can do justice in comparing anyone else to Jesus.

The best imitations are those that cannot be distinguished from the object being imitated. How far are you from looking like Jesus? Is your life a striking resemblance of Christ? What areas in your life would someone struggle to see you imitating Him?

Worshipper, get to know Jesus better! The better you know Christ, the better you can imitate Him. So study Him. Read about Him. Act like Him. Sing to Him. Pray to Him. Play music to Him. Study His Word. Examine what makes Him the most amazing role model in all of history and why no one else even comes close!

Question(s) of the Week: *What evidence is there in your life that God is truly your role model? Are you effectively imitating Him?*

Worship Leader: *Challenge your team: I want to challenge each of you to keep your earthly role models in check, including Christian artists, bands and songwriters.*

The Power of 1°

Matthew 27:50-54

50 And Jesus cried out again with a loud voice and yielded up his spirit.

51 And behold, the curtain of the temple was torn in two, from top to bottom. And the earth shook, and the rocks were split.

52 The tombs also were opened. And many bodies of the saints who had fallen asleep were raised,

53 and coming out of the tombs after his resurrection they went into the holy city and appeared to many.

54 When the centurion and those who were with him, keeping watch over Jesus, saw the earthquake and what took place, they were filled with awe and said, "Truly this was the Son of God!"

Picture it... The King of the Jews had been flogged, taunted and ridiculed. He was spit upon and crowned with thorns. A sign was placed above Him that said "King of the Jews" and the soldiers cast their lots for His clothing. He had just given up His life and now His lifeless body hung in plain sight for all to see.

Then some fascinating and incredible things happened. The curtain in the temple tore in two. The whole earth shook and the rocks split. Then a group of saints that had died were raised to life. They went into the city and appeared to many people. Imagine the sight! While there is much debate regarding the specifics of who these saints were, there is no doubt God made a profound statement through them.

Then there was the Centurion. He was a common soldier and a Gentile soldier at that. Notice God did not reveal Himself to His chosen people, the Jews, at this point. He revealed Himself to the hardest of Gentiles – a Roman soldier - a Centurion. When the Centurion and others around Him saw all that had happened, they acknowledged who Jesus truly was. One moment they were mocking and ridiculing Him; the next moment they were recognizing Him as the Son of God.

Have we grappled with the gravity of these moments in history? Do we understand the magnitude of what just happened here? Can we fathom the eternal ripple effect these events created? These miracles did not occur by accident, but rather, were intentionally placed by God Himself to show His power was not lost.

When we lead worship, do we recognize the infinite power of our Lord? Do we acknowledge that without Him we are unable to worship Him in spirit and in truth? Do we embrace the fact that He is the only one who can lead us into His presence through music? If God can raise His Son from the dead, raise others to march through the city, split curtains and rocks and cause earthquakes, He can certainly empower us to praise Him. Recognize it is through His power alone that we are able to lead anyone into His presence through worship.

Question(s) of the Week: *Do you try to lead others into God's presence through your own strength or through His?*

Worship Leader: *Pray now: Ask God to show His power to your team.*

―――――――――――――――――――――――――― ***The Power of 1°***

Daniel 3 (Portions)

1 King Nebuchadnezzar made an image of gold, whose height was sixty cubits and its breadth six cubits. He set it up on the plain of Dura, in the province of Babylon.

4 And the herald proclaimed aloud, "You are commanded, O peoples, nations, and languages,

5 that when you hear the sound of the horn, pipe, lyre, trigon, harp, bagpipe, and every kind of music, you are to fall down and worship the golden image that King Nebuchadnezzar has set up.

6 And whoever does not fall down and worship shall immediately be cast into a burning fiery furnace."

13 Then Nebuchadnezzar in furious rage commanded that Shadrach, Meshach, and Abednego be brought. So they brought these men before the king.

14 Nebuchadnezzar answered and said to them, "Is it true, O Shadrach, Meshach, and Abednego, that you do not serve my gods or worship the golden image that I have set up?

15 Now if you are ready when you hear the sound of the horn, pipe, lyre, trigon, harp, bagpipe, and every kind of music, to fall down and worship the image that I have made, well and good. But if you do not worship, you shall immediately be cast into a burning fiery furnace. And who is the god who will deliver you out of my hands?"

16 Shadrach, Meshach, and Abednego answered and said to the king, "O Nebuchadnezzar, we have no need to answer you in this matter.

17 If this be so, our God whom we serve is able to deliver us from the burning fiery furnace, and he will deliver us out of your hand, O king.

18 But if not, be it known to you, O king, that we will not serve your gods or worship the golden image that you have set up."

The law stated that when the symphony of music sounded, everyone in the land was to bow down and worship the king's golden image. Because of their disobedience to the king's edict, Shadrach, Meshach, and Abednego were thrown into a fiery furnace. A fourth man, *appearing like the Son of God,* was seen in the fire with them so King Nebuchadnezzar called the men out. Shadrach, Meshach and Abednego came out of the furnace not even smelling like smoke! King Nebuchadnezzar then commanded all of the land to worship the God of Shadrach, Meshach and Abednego.

Through faith, these three men took a stand against everyone around them – friends, family and neighbors - and broke the law by worshipping God. Think about it - wouldn't it have been easier to simply bow down to this false god *physically,* but *not mentally, emotionally* or *spiritually?* No one would have known. Besides, everyone else was doing it.

So why did they disobey? Were they just rebels? Did they have other motives?

God's laws always trump man's laws. In a world that is increasingly unaccepting of our Christian beliefs, ungodly rules and laws will follow that intrude on our ability to obey God's commands. We see this as our society constantly removes God's name from anything and everything it possibly can. We have seen this to a degree, but it will most likely continue to increase in scope and intensity until Christ returns.

Scripture specifically commands us as Christ followers and worshippers of God to obey *the laws of the land* unless it conflicts with God's laws (See Acts 5:27-29). As worshippers of Jesus Christ, you and I will most likely face persecution during our lives. There may be times we are told by people we cannot do what He commands us to do. How are you going to respond? Will you succumb to the pressures of the day as society attempts to confine God to a box? Or will you commit now to obey God at all costs? When pressures come, will your allegiance be to Christ above everything else?

Be careful to assess your heart and make your decision now. The cost may be high and the sacrifice may be great. But obeying God above all will never go in vain.

Question(s) of the Week: As worshippers, are you living now with a constant and unwavering faith?

Worship Leader: Pray now: Ask God to give your team the faith and resolve needed for any spiritual battle that comes their way.

_____ *The Power of 1°*

[Optional Materials: A popular hymn / worship song **]**

Mark 14:26

26 *And when they had sung a hymn, they went out to the Mount of Olives.*

The scene was in the evening in an upper room during Passover. Jesus was with His twelve closest friends, the disciples. To most of them, it was just an ordinary Passover meal. But to Jesus, they participated in the Lord's Supper together. Jesus broke bread and poured wine with His disciples representing His body and blood about to be broken and poured out on the cross. Other than Jesus, none of them knew the gravity of the moment. They had no concept that Jesus was about to be crucified. In fact, briefly after the meal, His friends were arguing over who should be considered the greatest among them. Despite all this, it was one of the most intimate times Jesus ever had with His disciples.

As they were wrapping up their last meal together, they did something very special. They sang a hymn. They all sang a song together and worshipped. Jesus worshipped with His disciples. Wow. He was about to go to the garden of Gethsemane to be betrayed and then crucified on a cross. But Jesus paused to worship through a song.

So why did they stop to sing a hymn? Did Peter have a good voice? Did they sing a traditional or new hymn? Was the volume too loud? How were the "acoustics" of the room? Did all of His disciples sing or did they stop to debate their personal worship preferences?

We may never know the answers to all of these questions, but one thing is for sure – they worshipped together. They took time in that moment to worship through song and did it within their local community of believers. Nothing else mattered. Worship style wasn't an issue. The quality of the singers was not scrutinized. Song selection or transitions were never mentioned. They simply worshipped.

Jesus was about to die for their sins and they paused to worship. When will we learn to worship God authentically in all circumstances without adding our own preferences and prejudices?

Question(s) of the Week: *Do you freely worship God out of a heart of gratitude and praise, or do your personal preferences get in the way?*

Worship Leader: *Sing now: Take time now to sing a hymn or worship song while reflecting on the night Jesus was with His disciples in the upper room.*

The Power of 1°

Make a Joyful Noise!

Psalm 100:1

1 *Make a joyful noise to the Lord, all the earth!*

Psalm 100 is a psalm of both praise and thanksgiving for who God is and what He has done for us. This verse is addressed to Christians throughout the earth. It is a strong invitation - a plea if you will - that all Christ followers are to make a joyful noise and direct it to the Lord.

But somehow many people have missed the real meaning here. This verse is often misunderstood to refer to our human desire for *pleasant sounding music*. That is not what this verse is referring to. This misconstrued thinking is reflected in comments like: *"It certainly doesn't sound like a joyful noise to me!"*

When God gives us a command like this, He always supplies a way for us to fulfill it with His help. Regardless of how well someone plays or sings, this verse more accurately refers to the *abundant joy* we possess and display as Christ followers. As believers we are to praise Him out of a deep, personal joy for the Lord. It is possible for poor quality music to be offered with an abundant amount of joy. In contrast, beautiful music can still be done without joy. God cares much more about the heart condition of the worshipper than He does the audible sounds being lifted up.

Anyone, even non-believers, can make *noise*. But only a life that has been changed through the blood of Christ can have any evidence of true joy, for joy is a fruit of the Spirit (See Galatians 5:22-23). This is further evidence that only Christians can make a joyful noise through Christ working in them. In response to the infinite depth of His love for us, He is deserving of at least this!

As Christians, we should worship our Lord out of a heart deeply filled with joy and gratitude. Do you worship out of a heart that is so full of joy for Christ that you feel compelled to praise Him? Does your joy permeate throughout your life to people in your family, neighborhood and work or do you save it for church only? Let your joy for the Lord be the catalyst by which you worship. Allow the Holy Spirit to fill every part of your life so your joy for Him shines out to others.

Question(s) of the Week: *Is your worship full of joy or is it just noise?*

Worship Leaders: *Encourage your team: Take a moment right now and reflect on the motivation of your heart in making a joyful noise.*

The Power of 1°

Psalms 100:2-5

2 Serve the Lord with gladness! Come into his presence with singing!

3 Know that the Lord, he is God! It is he who made us, and we are his; we are his people, and the sheep of his pasture.

4 Enter his gates with thanksgiving, and his courts with praise! Give thanks to him; bless his name!

5 For the Lord is good; his steadfast love endures forever, and his faithfulness to all generations.

David took every opportunity to express his love, praise and adoration toward God. As a shepherd, he had plenty of time in the fields to meditate and connect with His Lord. Imagine watching a flock of sheep every single day. Most days there would not be a lot of activity going on. But on occasion an animal, such as a bear or a lion, would prowl on the sheep. When this occurred David would kill the animal. As a shepherd, David became exceptional at two things: using a sling and praising God. It was a physical and spiritual training ground for him.

David is addressing all believers here and pointing us directly to the Lord. I'm going to read these verses again. Listen to all of the times David says *"he"* and *"his"* referring to God. *(Read the passage again now.)* Notice David didn't draw attention to himself here.

This invitation of exercising an attitude of praise extends to both our personal and corporate worship experiences. Whether we are in personal or corporate worship, we should come before Him and worship the Lord with gladness and joyful songs. David wrote this passage from His personal worship time with God. If we are worshipping throughout the week as David did, we will be equipped and ready to worship corporately. But if we come to church and have not been effectively worshipping personally during the week, our corporate worship will turn away from God and towards us. This is not what God ever intended. Worship is never about us. It is about ascribing glory to God with our hearts, minds and our very lives.

Do you follow His command to worship Him with a joyful heart or are you simply going through the *worship routine* each week? The time is now to worship God in His holiness. We should forget about ourselves and bring our gladness, thankfulness and joyful hearts to Him. He deserves it. It is up to us to respond in a manner that pleases Him.

Question(s) of the Week: *Are you praising God throughout the week or only on Sundays? Are you bringing your individual praise into corporate worship?*

Worship Leader: *Challenge your team: Please evaluate your personal worship experiences throughout the week to make sure your corporate worship is an overflow of your personal worship to the Lord.*

The Power of 1°

The Shell Game of Sin

Mark 10:17-22

17 And as he [Jesus] was setting out on his journey, a man ran up and knelt before him and asked him, "Good Teacher, what must I do to inherit eternal life?"

18 And Jesus said to him, "Why do you call me good? No one is good except God alone.

19 You know the commandments: 'Do not murder, Do not commit adultery, Do not steal, Do not bear false witness, Do not defraud, Honor your father and mother.'"

20 And he said to him, "Teacher, all these I have kept from my youth."

21 And Jesus, looking at him, loved him, and said to him, "You lack one thing: go, sell all that you have and give to the poor, and you will have treasure in heaven; and come, follow me."

22 Disheartened by the saying, he went away sorrowful, for he had great possessions.

1 Samuel 16:7b

7b "For the Lord sees not as man sees: man looks on the outward appearance, but the Lord looks on the heart."

Here we find a man running to kneel at Jesus' feet. He asks Jesus one simple question: "Good teacher, what must I do to inherit eternal life?" To answer the man's question, Jesus lists several sins he should avoid. The man replied: "Teacher, all *these I have kept from my youth."* While the young man's response was no doubt sincere, it was inaccurate.

Every child disobeys his parents at times. While this man may have been a great son growing up, he certainly disobeyed his parents occasionally, thereby not honoring them. And while this wealthy ruler never physically committed adultery, scripture states that if he had ever lusted after a woman he had committed adultery in his heart (Matthew 5:27-28). Additionally, his wealth was abundant and he had no desire to surrender his affluence for the sake of Christ. He only assessed his external sins rather than weighing his internal heart condition and surrendering everything to God.

Many churches, possibly ours, are full of people that spend more time assessing how others perceive them rather than how God sees them – in the internal, hidden places of their lives. People put on their *Sunday best* in front of others both in their attitudes as well as their actions. But internally, their minds and hearts are infected with all sorts of hidden sins. It's as if we are playing a shell game with our sin - If others don't see it, then it doesn't have to be addressed. Remember, God sees the deepest parts of us. He knows all things. Nothing is hidden from Him. His perspective should weigh heavier on us than anyone else. He is God and He is the only one we worship.

What about you... Are you holding anything back from God? Are you more concerned with man's viewpoint or God's perspective? Do you participate in worship each week while still harboring deep-rooted sin? God knows your thoughts and actions. Surrender everything to Him and address those areas He is bringing to your mind at this time.

Question(s) of the Week: *What parts of your hidden life are full of sin and need to be addressed? How are you going to correct these areas that are holding you back from authentic worship?*

Worship Leader: *Pray now: Ask God to reveal your team members' sins to them so they can repent and surrender everything to Him.*

The Power of 1°

Exodus 2:11-14

11 One day, when Moses had grown up, he went out to his people and looked on their burdens, and he saw an Egyptian beating a Hebrew, one of his people.

12 He looked this way and that, and seeing no one, he struck down the Egyptian and hid him in the sand.

13 When he went out the next day, behold, two Hebrews were struggling together. And he said to the man in the wrong, "Why do you strike your companion?"

14 He answered, "Who made you a prince and a judge over us? Do you mean to kill me as you killed the Egyptian?" Then Moses was afraid, and thought, "Surely the thing is known."

Exodus 3 (Portions)

1 Now Moses was keeping the flock of his father-in-law, Jethro, the priest of Midian, and he led his flock to the west side of the wilderness and came to Horeb, the mountain of God.

2 And the angel of the Lord appeared to him in a flame of fire out of the midst of a bush. He looked, and behold, the bush was burning, yet it was not consumed.

4 When the Lord saw that he turned aside to see, God called to him out of the bush, "Moses, Moses!" And he said, "Here I am."

10 *"Come, I will send you to Pharaoh that you may bring my people, the children of Israel, out of Egypt."*
11 *But Moses said to God, "Who am I that I should go to Pharaoh and bring the children of Israel out of Egypt?"*

Many men and women throughout the Bible had colossal failures. One such man was Moses. Although Moses grew up in the palace with the Egyptian royal family, God gave him a sensitive spirit towards God's people, the Israelites. After observing an Egyptian beating a Hebrew, Moses, in his unholy anger, killed the Egyptian. His sin caused damage to his fellowship with God. Since all sin is considered rebellion to a Holy God, Moses had a great need for restoration.

God didn't have to restore His fellowship with Moses, but He did. There was nothing Moses could do to restore this broken fellowship. Moses had a deficiency in his spiritual life that needed to be restored. Like a tattered and torn antique, restoration could only be done by the Master. God in His omnipotence is the only one that could mend this spiritual rift with Moses.

Through a burning bush, God took a meek and defeated Moses and raised him up to lead the Israelites out of Egypt. Even though he did not *feel qualified* whatsoever to do the task God had called him to do, God gently restored Moses to use him to do great things. God even brought Moses' brother, Aaron, alongside him to help him carry out the tasks that were beyond Moses' abilities.

We are like Moses in that we are just as much in need of restoration as he was. The weight of our sins would break any holy scale, were it not being sustained by the cross of Christ. In our deep depravity, only the redemption of Christ gives us hope, purpose and an eternal future. Through God and His infinite love for us, we have forgiveness and restoration from all of our sins.

You may not *feel qualified* to lead people in worship. You may believe you don't have the spiritual credentials necessary. Perhaps your past haunts you. Maybe your future looks bleak. God is still God. He wants to use you. Serve Him faithfully and let Him use you however He wishes. Through God's gentle restoration we can have success in ushering people into the presence of God.

Question(s) of the Week: *In what ways has God restored you from something, to ultimately plant you firmly where He wants you to be?*

Worship Leader: *Pray now: Thank God for His restoring power.*

_____ ***The Power of 1°***

Proverbs 14:30

30 A tranquil heart gives life to the flesh, but envy makes the bones rot.

Ecclesiastes 4:4

4 Then I saw that all toil and all skill in work come from a man's envy of his neighbor. This also is vanity and a striving after wind.

Envy is a common word used throughout scripture, but it's not as frequently used in today's society. Envy is wanting what someone else has and resenting them for having it. We can be envious of many things, such as money, possessions, status, relationships, personal characteristics, talents, musical skills and much more. Scripture tells us that a content, peaceful heart gives life, but envy rots us to the core!

Envy is one of the *sins of comparison*. Any time we compare ourselves to others, we begin the slippery slope of moving away from God's will and sinning. Scripture teaches us that being envious and pursuing what others possess is vanity and cannot be achieved; it is like chasing the wind.

Envy is also known as a *seed sin*. This is when one sin produces other sins such as unholy anger, fear and covetousness. Envy indicates we are not content with what God has blessed us with so we pursue what others have. This causes strain in our fellowship with God and other sins are soon to follow.

God desires for us to possess what He has given us to bring Him the greatest glory. Do you ever want what someone else possesses? Are you pleased with the talents God has entrusted to you? Are you content with the God-given musical abilities He has blessed you with or are you envious of others in our worship ministry? Stop. Pray right now and thank God that you don't have what others possess. God has uniquely equipped and blessed you with what He desires for you to have to bring Him the greatest glory.

Do you appreciate what God has given you? Then show satisfaction to Him in how He has blessed you. Display contentment toward God with the characteristics He has adorned you with. Express gratefulness to your Father for the possessions and wealth He has bestowed upon you. Desire nothing more than Him alone. You can't possess what everyone else has. Just remember, no one else possesses everything you have either.

Question(s) of the Week: *Who or what are you envious of?*

Worship Leader: *Pray now: Ask God to help you and your team to be content and pleased with the many blessings God has given you rather than desiring things you don't have.*

The Power of 1°

[Optional Materials: A 30-second timer **]**

Psalm 46:10a

10a *"Be still, and know that I am God."*

In this seemingly simple verse, there are two separate, yet profound commands: *"Be still"* and *"Know that I am God"*. First we are commanded to *"Be still"*. This doesn't mean to simply sit without moving – it means so much more. We should *still* both our bodies as well as our minds and try to remove external distractions, so our focus is exclusively on God.

This discipline of taking crevasses of time out of our chaotic lifestyles to reflect on God is becoming more and more scarce. But even more alarming than this is the lost practice of the second command: *"Know that I am God"*. Believing there is a god and knowing God personally are two entirely different things. Scripture says that even the demons believe there is a God and shudder (James 2:19). Knowing God deeply and more personally should be the life-long pursuit of every Christ follower. But in a world where life's demands are abundant and stress seems ever-present, this can be very difficult. Regardless, these two commands must be wrestled with until they become second nature in our lives.

Let's do something very practical... Let's take 30 seconds right now and think about God. I will time us, so you don't have to think about that. During these 30 seconds, don't sit idle and just wait for the time to end. Also, don't dwell on things going on in your life. Don't present requests. Just be still and think only about God. Meditate on God. Focus on the person and nature of God. Allow Him to speak and reveal Himself to you. Ready? Go. *(Wait 30 seconds here...)*

Stop. Were you able to invest 30 seconds of your life and think only about God? Did distracting thoughts come into your mind? What else did you think about, other than God? This discipline of being still and knowing He is God can be very challenging. Like any discipline, it takes an intentional, committed effort until the unnatural becomes natural in our lives. Let's each dedicate time daily to being still before our Lord and acknowledge who He really is.

Question(s) of the Week: *How are you doing in your personal life at being still and knowing He is God?*

Worship Leader: *Pray now: Pray for at least 60 seconds to give people a chance to be still before the Lord.*

_____ *The Power of 1°*

Colossians 3:23-24

23 *Whatever you do, work heartily, as for the Lord and not for men,*

24 *knowing that from the Lord you will receive the inheritance as your reward. You are serving the Lord Christ.*

Paul is giving instructions to the church at Colossae on how to live the Christian life. He is encouraging Christians to do their very best in whatever they do. Christians and non-Christians serve different "Masters" - While Christians serve Christ, non-Christians serve themselves. Because of this, there should be a distinct difference in what motivates us as believers compared to what motivates the world.

One place this should be evident is in our work ethic. If we do as this verse commands, our *working heartily* for the Lord will not diminish when we have a bad boss. It doesn't decline when the circumstances of life aren't going our way. It won't seek good for itself, but for others. It isn't affected when times get tough. It doesn't have a begrudging heart, but a cheerful one. The quality of our efforts should not change based on our circumstances or environment.

We all have responsibilities that aren't glamorous. It may be taking out the trash. It could include setting up chairs at church. Maybe it's something behind the scenes for our worship ministry. Regardless of what it is, we are to work heartily and do our best for the Lord.

Your job may not be fulfilling right now. Work with excellence because you are serving the Lord. Your spouse or kids may not be showing you the love and respect you need. Model love and respect toward them and let God deal with them regarding their response. You may not care for some of the songs we play and sing. Keep your heart steadfast on Christ, not on the music.

As part of our worship ministry, there are times you may not agree with the decisions being made. Likewise, there are times I may not agree with the decisions other people are making either. Regardless, this passage says we are to work heartily and give God our best, because He is the One we serve.

Are you working heartily for the Lord in our worship ministry? Do you give God your best at work, school and other activities or are you cutting corners in any way that would not be pleasing to God? Follow through on your commitment and work to honor God, not man.

Question(s) of the Week: *Are you working heartily for the Lord in everything you do?*

Worship Leader: *Pray now: Ask God to help you and your team members to give God your best efforts regardless of your circumstances.*

The Power of 1°

Luke 4:14-16

14 And Jesus returned in the power of the Spirit to Galilee, and a report about him went out through all the surrounding country.

15 And he taught in their synagogues, being glorified by all.

16 And he came to Nazareth, where he had been brought up. And as was his custom, he went to the synagogue on the Sabbath day, and he stood up to read.

Hebrews 10:24-25

24 And let us consider how to stir up one another to love and good works,

25 not neglecting to meet together, as is the habit of some, but encouraging one another, and all the more as you see the Day drawing near.

After Jesus wandered in the wilderness for forty days, He was tempted by Satan. Satan tempted Jesus three times and Jesus withstood each and every temptation. Then, Jesus started His earthly ministry and everything changed. In a sense, Jesus moved from *spiritual defense* to *spiritual offense*. Through the power of the Spirit, He taught in synagogues and was glorified and respected by all. At this point in His ministry, Jesus was not met with contempt or resistance, but with open arms. His reputation had preceded Him.

Jesus then went to Nazareth where He grew up and was well known. He attended the synagogue on the Sabbath where He stood and read. *(Now it was the custom of the day that there were seven readers in the synagogue every Sabbath: one Priest, one Levite and five other Israelites of that particular synagogue.)* Throughout the scriptures we find Jesus *preaching* in synagogues, but this is the only time He was found *reading* in a synagogue.

Here the scripture tells us something very interesting: it says *"as was His custom"*. Growing up, Jesus' practice was to attend the synagogue on the Sabbath. In other words, He regularly attended corporate worship! Not only did He attend, He actively invested in the lives of other believers around Him during worship. He attended. He worshipped. He led by reading. He engaged with His local body of believers and worshipped along with them.

Since Jesus went to worship on a regular basis, we should do the same by consistently participating in corporate worship. We should also actively invest in the lives of people within our local body of believers. This includes encouraging others and helping them grow in their relationship with Christ *(Hebrews 10:24-25)*. Jesus set these examples for us. It is up to us to follow His lead.

Question(s) of the Week: *When you think about your personal worship, is God pleased with your level of* engagement? Are you "worshipping regularly" or simply "going through the motions" each week?

Worship Leader: Pray now: Ask God to help you and your team to be faithful in worshipping together and in encouraging others to grow in their relationship with Christ.

_____ *The Power of 1°*

[Optional Materials: A broom **]**

Luke 10:38-42

38 Now as they went on their way, Jesus entered a village. And a woman named Martha welcomed him into her house.

39 And she had a sister called Mary, who sat at the Lord's feet and listened to his teaching.

40 But Martha was distracted with much serving. And she went up to him and said, "Lord, do you not care that my sister has left me to serve alone? Tell her then to help me."

41 But the Lord answered her, "Martha, Martha, you are anxious and troubled about many things,

42 but one thing is necessary. Mary has chosen the good portion, which will not be taken away from her."

Jesus visited Mary and Martha frequently. Scripture tells us that on this particular occasion, Mary sat down at Jesus' feet and listened to Him teach. Mary was worshipping and communing with her Lord. She was fixated on every word He spoke. She observed every gesture He made. She had absolutely no agenda, but to spend time with Jesus and listen. She was still. She was quiet. She was soaking it all in.

Martha was a very different story. She was busy taking care of the household chores. She was not focused on anything but the work right before her. While her intentions of taking care of the tasks were noble and good, she was distracted from what was best.

Martha's attitude festered. She was getting very irritated with her sister Mary. Frustrating questions were likely swirling in her head regarding why she was the only one *working* while Mary was just sitting down. Questions like: *"Why can't Mary help me so we can both chat with Jesus?"* most certainly were entertained by Martha.

Jesus' response to Martha was loving, but direct. It was compassionate but deafening. In fact, he says Martha's name twice for emphasis. He goes on to acknowledge her work, as well as her attitude. He essentially tells Martha that she is busy with good things but is distracted from the best thing, which would have been listening to Jesus and communing with Him.

Even though Jesus was a frequent guest of theirs, He did not compromise in keeping His eyes on God and revealing to them what God desires. He spoke the truth in love. He encouraged Mary to continue investing time with Him while encouraging Martha to do the same.

How about you? Is your *service* to the Lord taking priority over your *relationship* with Him? Whether it's serving in our worship ministry or another area of the church, your service to Him should always be secondary to your relationship with Him. Martha missed the moment with Jesus because of her desire to serve the immediate needs of the day. We should be cautious to avoid doing the same.

Question(s) of the Week: *How is your busy schedule distracting you from "sitting at Jesus' feet", listening to Him and worshipping Him?*

Worship Leader: *Pray now: Pray that your team will never get so busy that God is not priority #1 in their lives.*

_____ ***The Power of 1°***

Matthew 12:9-14

9 *He went on from there and entered their synagogue*

10 *And a man was there with a withered hand. And they asked him, "Is it lawful to heal on the Sabbath?" - so that they might accuse him.*

11 *He said to them, "Which one of you who has a sheep, if it falls into a pit on the Sabbath, will not take hold of it and lift it out?*

12 *Of how much more value is a man than a sheep! So it is lawful to do good on the Sabbath."*

13 *Then he said to the man, "Stretch out your hand." And the man stretched it out, and it was restored, healthy like the other.*

14 *But the Pharisees went out and conspired against him, how to destroy him.*

The Pharisees and religious leaders were attempting to trap Jesus. Their Pharisaical laws classified healing people on the Sabbath as *working* and they considered it forbidden. The problem was that this was not God's law. They placed greater value on their own religious practices rather than their relationship with Jesus. Since their attention was on their rules rather than on God, Jesus revealed their misplaced devotion and pointed them back to Him. It's interesting to note that we have no indication the man with the withered hand ever asked to be healed. This healing took place to correct the Pharisees' improper traditions and to demonstrate Jesus' omnipotence.

Jesus provoked the legalists of His day. He did this when He called the religious rulers *hypocrites* on multiple occasions. Going a step further, Jesus violated the legalistic rules of the Pharisees to the point of offending them. He denounced stoning the woman caught in adultery (John 8:1-11). He also healed on the Sabbath on two separate occasions. First, the man with the withered hand and second, the crippled woman that had a disabling spirit for 18 years (Luke 13:10-17).

Legalism emphasizes the external perceptions of people while neglecting the internal heart condition. It elevates the action over the motivation of the action. This was commonly seen among the religious leaders of Jesus' day. For example: Was it the murderers and adulterers that put Jesus on the cross? No, it was the legalistic chief priests and rulers.

Is there legalism in your life? Do you hold your own personal preferences and traditions higher than what God's Word teaches? Do you value what your parents taught you in greater esteem than what your Heavenly Father has revealed to you? Be careful you are not falling into the trap of legalism.

Also, if you notice any legalism occurring in our worship ministry, please let us know so we can address it. Legalism can destroy churches and worship teams. Let's work together to make sure we are God-honoring in all we say and do.

Question(s) of the Week: *Have you become legalistic in any way? Are you more focused on following Christian rules or following God?*

Worship Leader: *Ask your team: What are some areas where we, as Christians, have a tendency to become legalistic?*

———————————————————————— **The Power of 1°**

Mark 9:20-24

20 And they brought the boy to him. And when the spirit saw him, immediately it convulsed the boy, and he fell on the ground and rolled about, foaming at the mouth.

21 And Jesus asked his father, *"How long has this been happening to him?"* And he said, "From childhood.

22 And it has often cast him into fire and into water, to destroy him. But if you can do anything, have compassion on us and help us."

23 And Jesus said to him, *"'If you can'! All things are possible for one who believes."*

24 Immediately the father of the child cried out and said, "I believe; help my unbelief!"

Here we find a desperate father in need of extravagant help. His son has been demon-possessed since childhood. For years, the child was relentlessly thrown into fires and bodies of water by the demon trying to destroy the child. But God sustained the boy for such a time as this. Out of agony, exhaustion and despair, the father goes to Jesus hoping He can do something. He wasn't just asking for help for his son, but for himself as well, indicated by him saying *"take pity on us and help us"*.

The father asked Jesus for compassion and help. Not being certain if Jesus could or would help, this man cried out in desperation. He was honest and transparent – his faith wasn't strong enough to state confidently that Jesus could take care of this issue. His faith was weak regarding these circumstances. Yet he brought all the faith he had and relied on Jesus to provide the rest.

If we are truly honest with ourselves, we face similar faith challenges at times. We want to believe God can take care of anything but when we face deep wounds and personal challenges, many of us lack the spiritual fortitude to go through life's trials with complete faith in our Heavenly Father. He brings us through these experiences in our lives so we have the opportunity to grow in our faith. This is where sanctification intersects with our humanity – God strengthens us and increases our faith through these life-altering experiences.

We are not born with this faith. We cannot create this faith on our own. This is the work of the Holy Spirit in us. This is where our lives converge with God's divine direction to lead us into becoming more like Him. As our faith grows, our love and understanding of God grows along with it, enabling us to worship Him in a deeper, more authentic way. God ultimately desires for us, as His worshippers, to grow into having full and complete faith in Him; *"for without faith it is impossible to please God"* (Heb. 11:6).

Question(s) of the Week: What circumstances are you currently facing where your faith is being challenged? Have you asked God to increase your faith during these trials?

Worship Leader: Ask your team: Would any of you feel comfortable sharing examples of how God is stretching and growing your faith?

———————————————————————— **The Power of 1°**

Mark 9:25-29

25 And when Jesus saw that a crowd came running together, he rebuked the unclean spirit, saying to it, *"You mute and deaf spirit, I command you, come out of him and never enter him again."*

26 And after crying out and convulsing him terribly, it came out, and the boy was like a corpse, so that most of them said, "He is dead."

27 But Jesus took him by the hand and lifted him up, and he arose.

28 And when he had entered the house, his disciples asked him privately, "Why could we not cast it out?"

29 And he said to them, *"This kind cannot be driven out by anything but prayer."*

Jesus makes a point here to name the unclean spirit by its debilitating treatment of this boy, calling it a *"mute and deaf spirit"*. Jesus didn't mince words with the spirit. When He called out the demon, He told the demon to come out of the boy and never enter him again. Jesus never did anything second-rate and, true to His nature, He certainly didn't here.

Interestingly, the demon did not come out without a fight. Before it left the boy, it threw him to and fro, convulsing him violently. Finally the demon left the boy lying there lifeless. It was said by eyewitnesses that *he was dead.* The boy did not move. But again, Jesus didn't do anything halfway. He not only commanded the demon to come out of the boy, he also raised the lifeless boy up.

While Jesus' disciples tried to cast this demon out, they could not. Notice here that when the disciples asked Jesus privately why they couldn't cast the demon out, He didn't say it wasn't possible for them to do so. Jesus simply pointed them to God and His power, which He provides through prayer. All power comes from God. Prayer is how we maintain our communication with Him and tap into His power. Jesus went to His Father in prayer to gain the strength needed to do this miracle.

As worship leaders and team members, if we aren't focused on God in our Christian walk, we can become complacent and begin trusting in our own abilities rather than in God, just as the disciples did. We become powerless when our reliance on God fades. If kept unchecked, we can go through the motions of our Christian life for years and rely only on our own strength instead of on God's omnipotent power.

This is exactly what the disciples did. They began believing in their own abilities rather than going to their Heavenly Father for their strength. Be careful to faithfully recognize that all of your power comes from God alone, not from your experiences or successes. Your musical talents and abilities are a product of His design, not your own choosing. Pray that God will continue to bless our ministry. Only God can empower and enable us as we face spiritual challenges ahead.

Question(s) of the Week: *Are you relying on your own strength and experiences in your Christian walk, or on God's divine power?*

Worship Leader: *Pray now: Ask God to strengthen your team's commitment to praying and relying on Him.*

--- *The Power of 1°*

Luke 5:15-16

15 But now even more the report about him went abroad, and great crowds gathered to hear him and to be healed of their infirmities.

16 But he would withdraw to desolate places and pray.

Jesus had the opportunity to speak here to a large crowd about the message of God's redemption and to heal many, many people. The crowd was not only open to the message of Jesus, but they gathered specifically to hear Him and to be healed of their infirmities. The disciples back then and even Christian leaders today would be *dying* for an opportunity like this! So why did Jesus just walk away? Was He being insensitive to the ministry opportunities around Him? How could He seemingly ignore the needs of these people?

Even when Jesus had crowds of people all around Him, He knew He had to intentionally maintain a vibrant fellowship with His Father. He was keenly aware of where His power came from. Without knowing the will of His Father, Jesus knew His human efforts and abilities would fail Him in meeting the real needs of these people and others.

Let's flash forward roughly 2,000 years. In today's society, life can be a blur. Between doctor's appointments, work obligations, family activities, sporting events, home repairs, worship team practices and other church responsibilities, there is very little *free time* in our lives. Regardless, escaping our self-inflicted busy schedules is difficult, but necessary.

To personally worship and lead others into the presence of God, we must constantly be in fellowship and communication with our power source, which is God. To do this, many of us tend to *carve out* time in our busy schedules when we can find a few extra minutes. Instead of squeezing God into our daily agendas, what if we started each day with a blank slate of time and placed God as our highest priority? Is He truly the most important part of our lives or is He just an after-thought?

Consider your own life for a moment. Are you a *carver*? Do you tend to carve out time for God? Rather than carving out time for Him here and there, give Him top priority in your life. Do what Jesus did. Practice *getting away* with God and watch Him take care of all the details of your life. Both you and God will be pleased with the results.

Question(s) of the Week: *Do you 'carve' out time to spend with God or is He the greatest priority in your life?*

Worship Leader: *Challenge your team: Consider personally tracking your time with God this week and evaluate the quality and amount of time you spend with Him. Make the necessary changes as appropriate.*

The Power of 1°

John 2:13-16

13 *The Passover of the Jews was at hand, and Jesus went up to Jerusalem.*

14 *In the temple he found those who were selling oxen and sheep and pigeons, and the money-changers sitting there.*

15 *And making a whip of cords, he drove them all out of the temple, with the sheep and oxen. And he poured out the coins of the money-changers and overturned their tables.*

16 *And he told those who sold the pigeons, "Take these things away; do not make my Father's house a house of trade."*

The priests and others in the temple committed two sins here. First, they were using designated animals for unholy purposes. These pigeons, sheep and other animals were reserved for anyone coming to the temple to offer a sacrifice to the Lord, not for buying and selling. Second, they were using the house of worship for irreverent activities in a place reserved exclusively for worship to God. The temple was a holy place, set aside for a holy purpose. Unholy activities such as these were not welcome here.

Jesus' response was instigated by the disgraceful activities occurring in the temple. In His righteous indignation, Jesus made a whip out of cords and drove out the unrighteous and unholy events taking place. Jesus demonstrated His passion and resolve for keeping His house and all that is His, absolutely holy. He did not compromise in any way the holiness of what was set apart for God alone. Jesus "cleaned house" to make sure His house was clean before God.

Where do we need to "clean house" in our church? Have you observed activities or behaviors that need to be addressed and corrected? What is the best way for us to deal with these issues in a God-honoring way? Spiritual compromise drives a wedge between us and our fellowship with God. Any unholy activity can greatly affect our ability to clearly hear God's voice as we lead others in worship. We must know God's precepts so we can defend them when they are being misused or violated. As worshippers of our Lord, we need to work together to protect the holy and sacred elements of our church so we can effectively follow Him and point people to Christ.

Question(s) of the Week: *Are there unholy activities occurring in our church that need to be addressed? How have we become complacent in our response to sinful activities around us?*

Worship Leader: *Pray Now: Ask God to give you and your team boldness in addressing anything within your church that is unholy so it can be addressed and corrected.*

The Power of 1°

Matthew 5:5

5 *"Blessed are the meek, for they shall inherit the earth."*

Meekness is one of the greatest, most under-appreciated character qualities throughout all of scripture. Unlike what some believe, meekness is nothing like weakness. In fact, the only thing they have in common is that they rhyme. Meekness can be thought of as *possessing power while exercising restraint*. It's also commonly referred to as *strength under control*.

Meekness does not defend its actions. When being attacked by others, it lets God be their defense. A meek person will tend to forgive many times over before even considering revenge or retaliation. As believers, when we live a life of meekness we actually surrender our right to be in control and let God rule our lives.

This verse indicates that people who are meek will enjoy their time on earth. They are blessed because they rarely have regrets in how they handle difficult situations. Think about it – if you and I were giving gentle responses to others (Proverbs 15:1) and not stirring up conflict, wouldn't our lives be more peaceful and Godly?

Jesus was the perfect example of meekness. He had unlimited power, but only drew upon it when directed by His Heavenly Father. He had all the strength necessary for any task, but exercised control in using His omnipotence. For example, He could have kept Lazarus from dying, but He chose not to. He was able to call legions of angels down to take Him off the cross, but He didn't. He had the ability to speak one word while He was in the wilderness and avoid even being tempted by Satan, but He refused to stop short of full obedience to God.

As worshippers and worship leaders, we should be the meekest people in the world. We should exercise self-control while maintaining access to the greatest power in the entire universe. There is no limit to the strength we possess through Christ. Yet we sometimes expect God to live within our human limitations. He never will though. It is not in His nature to live a powerless life when He is omnipotent.

Question(s) of the Week: *Are you living a life of meekness while tapping into the strength of Christ? Are you living under His control or your own?*

Worship Leader: *Ask your team: Would others perceive our overall worship ministry as meek and humble? Why or why not?*

———————————————————————— ***The Power of 1°***

1 Chronicles 16 (Portions)

23 Sing to the Lord, all the earth! Tell of his salvation from day to day.

24 Declare his glory among the nations, his marvelous works among all the peoples!

25 For great is the Lord, and greatly to be praised, and he is to be feared above all gods.

27 Splendor and majesty are before him; strength and joy are in his place.

28 Ascribe to the Lord, O families of the peoples, ascribe to the Lord glory and strength!

31 Let the heavens be glad, and let the earth rejoice, and let them say among the nations, "The Lord reigns!"

32 Let the sea roar, and all that fills it; let the field exult, and everything in it!

34 Oh give thanks to the Lord, for he is good; for his steadfast love endures forever!

36 "Blessed be the Lord, the God of Israel, from everlasting to everlasting!" Then all the people said, "Amen!" and praised the Lord.

Wow. This passage is a declaration, command and exaltation all wrapped up in one. It is abundant in bringing praise and glory to God. Its portrayal is only a glimpse of what God's vast worth really is. Words are too finite in even attempting to describe the infinite nature of our God; yet this passage endeavors to do so. Interestingly, the message here is delivered to God's people, but the praise and adoration is focused directly toward God.

While this powerful message was written so majestically during its day, rarely today do we hear such personal passion for the Lord. Why is this the case? Is He not worthy of greatly being praised? Is God no longer deserving of glory? Is He any less majestic now than He was when this was written? Has God ceased moving in the lives of Christians today compared to that of previous generations?

Regardless of people's beliefs and opinions, God is still God. He is still majestic. His love will endure forever. He is great and greatly to be praised. Every knee will bow before Him. Even rivers will clap their hands, hills will sing for joy (Psalm 98:8) and stones will cry out (Luke 19:40) in worship and adoration to Almighty God. He will ultimately be worshipped by everything, both on earth and in the heavens.

So as worshippers of the Living God, we should acknowledge Him in everything we do. He is our Lord. Let Him be Lord over your life. He is our Master. Be His servant. He has a heavenly agenda for us. Allow him to direct your calendar. He is the provider of all things. Let Him be the manager of the finances He has entrusted to you. He has plans for your life that are far greater than you can possibly imagine. Allow Him to be your personal life coach.

Question(s) of the Week: *Do you declare God's glory in all you say and do? Do you give Him the freedom to move in your life at all times?*

Worship Leader: *Ask your team: What characteristics of God mean the most to you personally, right now?*

——————————————————————— **The Power of 1°**

Mark 10:42-45

42 And Jesus called them to him and said to them, "You know that those who are considered rulers of the Gentiles lord it over them, and their great ones exercise authority over them.

43 But it shall not be so among you. But whoever would be great among you must be your servant,

44 and whoever would be first among you must be slave of all.

45 For even the Son of Man came not to be served but to serve, and to give his life as a ransom for many."

Because of their authority, Gentile leaders were lording over people. They were elevating themselves above others and looking down upon everyone around them. This should never be. Jesus is drawing a stark comparison here in this passage. He is contrasting Gentile leaders and their domination over others to what they should be, which are servant leaders.

It seems so contradictory, doesn't it - to serve and lead at the same time? Ordinary thinking of leading is that others serve you. But there is nothing ordinary about Jesus. In fact, He turned ordinary thinking upside down. Jesus was the ultimate servant leader. Yes, He led, but He did so by serving others through obedience to His Heavenly Father.

Jesus had no personal gain from healing the leper. He didn't get paid for calming the sea. He wasn't elevated politically for feeding 5,000 men and their families. He didn't become wealthy by having Peter catch a fish with a coin in its mouth to pay a tax. Jesus did all of these things and so much more through the heart of a servant leader.

His ultimate act of servant leadership was in obeying His Father by dying on the cross. His personal gain wasn't achieved in human power, but through physical pain. It wasn't realized in prestige, but through persecution. It didn't produce immediate praise, but personal rejection by His closest friends.

A clear indication that someone is a mature worshipper is when they lead as a servant. They are willing to do anything necessary to bring glory to God. No job is too small. No task is too minuscule. Servant leaders never view anything as below them. Jesus didn't either. Heaven's Hero broke through, abandoned His throne and entered the world as the perfect Servant Leader.

Are you serving in our worship ministry as a servant leader or by *leading servants* around you? Do you serve others by helping them achieve what God is calling them to accomplish? Or are you seeking to find people to come around you to serve you? Lead by example. Lead like Jesus did. Be a servant leader.

Question(s) of the Week: *Are you a leader of servants or a servant leader? What are some examples of people being effective servant leaders in our worship ministry?*

Worship Leader: *Ask your team: What are some ways you can improve in being an effective servant leader?*

_____ **The Power of 1°**

2 Corinthians 10:5b

5b *Take every thought captive to obey Christ.*

As worship leaders, team members and artists in our own right, God has given us the precious gift of creativity. It is a powerful gift and one that should be managed carefully. With creativity comes imagination and as musicians, we tend to have more than the average person. When creativity is left untamed, abuse sets in.

God wants us to exercise self-control both in our external activities as well as our inner-most thoughts. Every sin begins in the mind. If sinful thoughts enter our minds unchecked, they can wreak havoc and permeate throughout every area of our lives. But if we carefully and consistently practice taking every thought captive, Satan loses his power over us and we are able to faithfully follow God.

When scripture tells us to take every thought captive to Christ, it applies to what we should focus on as well as what we should avoid thinking about. The Apostle Paul tells us to think about whatever is honorable, pure, and anything worthy of praise (Phil. 4:8) while avoiding slander, sexual immorality, obscene talk and lying (Col 3:2-10).

Another area to keep in check is lust. Lust is *having an unbridled desire* and can apply to anything. It could be for a person you are not married to. Or for the latest technological gadget you must have right now. It could also be for a car, boat, prestige, money, fame and more.

To help guard against temptations of the mind we may need to install *spiritual hedges* to keep our minds under the Lordship of Christ. Spiritual hedges consist of many things, including: participating in Life Groups, Bible Studies, guarded television and movie watching, accountability partners and much more. Christ calls us to keep our thoughts in check because He knows they end up manifesting themselves into actions.

How are your thoughts these days? Are you allowing sinful thoughts to easily infiltrate your mind? Are you taking every thought captive? Has unhealthy creativity and imagination taken over in your mind? What spiritual hedges do you need to put in place to guard your mind and your spiritual walk? Capture your thoughts and surrender them to the Lord.

Question(s) of the Week: *Do you control your thoughts or do your thoughts control you?*

Worship Leader: *Pray now: Ask God to convict each team member regarding any ungodly thoughts so they can confess and turn away from their sin.*

The Power of 1°

Matthew 16:24

24 Then Jesus told his disciples, "If anyone would come after me, let him deny himself and take up his cross and follow me."

Jesus is telling His followers that if they truly want to be His disciples, they have to deny themselves, bear the burdens of Christ and pursue only Him. To do as this verse suggests, we have to surrender everything – even our own desires. Denying ourselves and following God is an intentional choice we must continually make as we worship our Lord. This includes denying the desires of our own human nature to satisfy the cravings of our soul. We cannot follow Him and pursue our own desires at the same time. We must wave the white flag of surrender to our Master and maintain this as our daily posture.

Everyone has desires. Desires by themselves are morally neutral, meaning they are neither good nor bad. For example, if a desire is inspired by God, it is healthy and spiritually beneficial. However, if it is our own desire without His guidance and inspiration, it is unhealthy and can be harmful to us and others.

Jesus, our Master, relentlessly modeled denying Himself. Humanly speaking, He didn't wish to die on the cross but He intentionally obeyed His Father's commands. He had no desire to be mocked and wear a crown of thorns but He allowed it to be pressed into His head. He wouldn't have personally chosen to be spit upon and beaten nearly to death, but through His great love for us He permitted it. He denied His own human preferences and surrendered His will to do His Father's will. We should do the same.

We all like to be in control – especially musicians! We have a natural propensity to believe we have all the right answers, don't we? Once we recognize the foolishness of our thinking and begin to deny our own desires, God can take control of our lives and make us into who He has created us to be. You and I can never deny ourselves too much in our pursuit of submitting to God's will. So deny yourself, take up His cross, follow Him and watch Him take you to spiritual places beyond your wildest dreams!

Question(s) of the Week: *In your life, where do you need to relinquish control to God?*

Worship Leader: *Pray now: Pray that you and your team will grow in the discipline of denying yourselves and following the Lord.*

The Power of 1°

Matthew 23:23

23 *"Woe to you, scribes and Pharisees, hypocrites! For you tithe mint and dill and cumin, and have neglected the weightier matters of the law: justice and mercy and faithfulness. These you ought to have done, without neglecting the others."*

Once again Jesus is correcting the scribes and Pharisees for their misplaced priorities of the law. He points out that the religious rulers were strict in obeying the lesser laws such as tithing*, while completely neglecting the greater laws, such as justice, mercy and faithfulness. In other words, they were majoring on the minor laws and minoring on the major ones!

Notice Jesus didn't say to stop tithing. The Pharisees were right to continue bringing their tithes to the Lord. Their error was in neglecting the intent of the law in exercising *justice, mercy and faithfulness*. They were more interested in following the legalistic commands while forsaking *"loving their neighbors as themselves"* (Mark 12:31).

It's easy for us as worship leaders and team members to also major on the minor things, isn't it? We ask questions like: *"Why did she get the solo?"*, *"Is that the best they can do?"*, *"Why are the worship practices so long?"*, *"Do we have to* sing that song again?", "Why don't we sing more hymns?" and "When are we going to play a new song?".

As Christ followers, we need to grow beyond these self-seeking questions and ask more mature ones. Questions like: "Am I truly worshipping God today?", "Am I sharing the gospel every opportunity I am given?", "Is my life looking more like Jesus?" and "How can I help others grow closer to Christ?".

Relating to worship, how do we know if we are on the right path? Is there a way to differentiate between the less important and more important matters? The answer is "yes". Our relationship with our Heavenly Father should be our only target. When our attention is focused less on the musical aspects and more on Jesus Christ, we know we are headed in the right direction. Does this describe you?

* Tithing was not done solely with money (such as denarii) but also with possessions, such as herbs and vegetables.

Question(s) of the Week: Are you majoring on the minor things and minoring on the major ones? Is your attention focused on Christ, or less significant matters?

Worship Leader: Challenge your team: Challenge them to check their attention to make sure it is fixed on Christ. Ask them to encourage others to do the same.

_____ **The Power of 1°**

2 Corinthians 12:7b-10

7b A thorn was given me in the flesh, a messenger of Satan to harass me, to keep me from becoming conceited.

8 Three times I pleaded with the Lord about this, that it should leave me.

9 But he said to me, "My grace is sufficient for you, for my power is made perfect in weakness." Therefore I will boast all the more gladly of my weaknesses, so that the power of Christ may rest upon me.

10 For the sake of Christ, then, I am content with weaknesses, insults, hardships, persecutions, and calamities. For when I am weak, then I am strong.

Paul's *thorn in the flesh* absolutely tormented him. There has been a lot of speculation about what this thorn actually was, but Paul understood its purpose was to keep him humble. Yes it was both a bother and a distraction, but Paul embraced God's grace and did not let this limitation deter him from being fully used by God.

Throughout scripture, men and women alike faced obstacles and limitations. Moses stuttered. David committed adultery. The disciples were not extremely intelligent. Rahab was a prostitute. Samson became weak to a woman in spite of his physical strength. Jonah ran from God. Saul killed Christians. Peter was impulsive. Noah got drunk. Yet all of these people did incredible things for the kingdom of God as they overcame their own personal challenges, impediments and weaknesses.

Noah was faithful in obeying God and building the ark. Moses led the Exodus out of Egypt. David became an amazing king. The disciples were pillars of the early church. Rahab protected two Jewish spies in their desperate time of need. Samson, despite losing his sight, destroyed more Philistines at his death than throughout his entire life. Jonah led the people of Nineveh to repent before God. Saul, becoming Paul upon his conversion, wrote much of the New Testament. Peter was a great apostle to the Jews.

Throughout history, God used the weaknesses of His people to accomplish great things. The same is true today. You may not be the best singer. There may be better instrumentalists in the church or at least in this area than you. You may be younger or less experienced than others. Maybe you haven't been a Christian very long. Perhaps you feel you are too old. You may have a sketchy past.

Regardless of your limitations, weaknesses and obstacles, God deserves your very best. Depend on Him to take you where you are at and use you for greater purposes than you can imagine and accomplish on your own. Everyone has limitations. Do not let your limitations be an excuse for mediocrity.

Question(s) of the Week: *Where are you letting your limitations keep you from giving God your best?*

Worship Leader: *Ask your team: Do you see specific areas where our limitations as a team and church have taken over and mediocrity has set in?*

––––––––––––––––––––––––––––––––– **The Power of 1°**

God, an Old Man and a Young Lad

1 Samuel 3:4-10

4 Then the Lord called Samuel, and he said, "Here I am!"

5 and ran to Eli and said, "Here I am, for you called me." But he said, "I did not call; lie down again." So he went and lay down.

6 And the Lord called again, "Samuel!" and Samuel arose and went to Eli and said, "Here I am, for you called me." But he said, "I did not call, my son; lie down again."

7 Now Samuel did not yet know the Lord, and the word of the Lord had not yet been revealed to him.

8 And the Lord called Samuel again the third time. And he arose and went to Eli and said, "Here I am, for you called me." Then Eli perceived that the Lord was calling the boy.

9 Therefore Eli said to Samuel, "Go, lie down, and if he calls you, you shall say, 'Speak, Lord, for your servant hears.'" So Samuel went and lay down in his place.

10 And the Lord came and stood, calling as at other times, "Samuel! Samuel!" And Samuel said, "Speak, for your servant hears."

Eli's sons were a mess. They showed contempt for sacrifices to the Lord and did detestable things with women at the entrance to the tent of meeting (1 Samuel 2:17, 22). While his own sons were far from God, another young man close to Eli was being raised up by the Lord – Samuel. Samuel was

God's chosen servant to obey God and do what was in God's heart and mind (1 Samuel 2:35).

While Samuel was lying down, he heard a voice and thought it was Eli. Eli told the boy twice that he wasn't calling for him and to go lie back down. The third time, Eli realized it was the Lord calling. So when the Lord called a fourth time for Samuel, he responded just as Eli instructed: *"Speak, Lord, for your servant hears."* It's important to note that God initiated the conversation and relationship with Samuel rather than Samuel pursuing God.

Eli didn't try to interpret what God wanted to say to Samuel - He simply redirected Samuel back to the Lord. Also, God did not speak through Eli - He spoke directly to Samuel. In response, Samuel didn't second guess it was the Lord speaking or create *spiritual hoops* for God to jump through to confirm it was really Him. After hearing from God, Samuel didn't need Eli's confirmation that what he understood from God was accurate – Samuel simply trusted God.

As worshippers called to lead others into the presence of God, we should approach God first to gain direction before going to anyone else. However, many of us are quick to go to our closest friends, spiritual advisors and other believers to confirm God is truly speaking to us. Why don't we go straight to God first? Why would we trust imperfect people over an omnipotent God?

God is not a God of confusion but a God of clarity. We need to learn to trust Him above all else. There is no one that knows what we need more than God. We are to grow in our faith in Him so we can worship Him in deeper ways and lead others to do the same. Seek Him first, before anyone else (Matt 6:33). Trust in Him, not in your own common sense and He will direct your paths (Proverbs 3:5-6).

Question(s) of the Week: *Who do you go to first for advice and counsel: God, or other people?*

Worship Leader: *Challenge your team: This week, be aware of how often you seek someone else's advice before going to God.*

_____ ***The Power of 1°***

Genesis 22:1-5

1 After these things God tested Abraham and said to him, "Abraham!" And he said, "Here I am."

2 He said, "Take your son, your only son Isaac, whom you love, and go to the land of Moriah, and offer him there as a burnt offering on one of the mountains of which I shall tell you."

3 So Abraham rose early in the morning, saddled his donkey, and took two of his young men with him, and his son Isaac. And he cut the wood for the burnt offering and arose and went to the place of which God had told him.

4 On the third day Abraham lifted up his eyes and saw the place from afar.

5 Then Abraham said to his young men, "Stay here with the donkey; I and the boy will go over there and worship and come again to you."

God gave Abraham clear directions to take his only son Isaac and sacrifice him as a burnt offering. To put this in context, this is the same son that God gave Abraham when he was 100 years old and Sarah, when she was 90! God had already promised that Abraham's offspring would be as numerous as the stars. So how could a loving God ask for such a thing? With all these facts, God still commanded Abraham to sacrifice his one and only beloved son.

God didn't tell Abraham right away which mountain to go to - He simply said to go to the region of Moriah and He would tell him which mountain to make the sacrifice on. So Abraham woke up early the next morning and didn't delay in obeying God. He took two servants, his son Isaac and a donkey on the trip. After three days into the journey, Abraham looked up and saw, off in the distance, where God was leading them. Scripture doesn't indicate what Abraham actually thought during his three-day journey but I wonder: Did Abraham question how God was going to protect his son and fulfill His promise? Was God going to bring Isaac back to life? Was something surprising and extraordinary going to take place during their three days of travel?

Abraham's faith remained steadfast the entire time. He didn't question God or His commands. He told his servants to stay with the donkey. He then said he and his son would go worship and *they* would come back. Wow. He didn't tell his servants he was going to sacrifice Isaac. He simply said *"We will worship and then we will come back to you."* In obedience Abraham went to worship God. He knew God would fulfill His promise to make him the father of many nations.

As Christ followers, there are times when our steps will defy human logic. This is where faith comes in. When God leads us, we should trust Him rather than ourselves and our limited perspective. Are you willing to do as Abraham did and walk by faith rather than sight? Or will you limit God's activity in your life to operate only as far as your finite human understanding can reach?

Question(s) of the Week: How is God asking you to step out in faith? Will you respond in immediate obedience as Abraham did?

Worship Leader: Challenge your team: Assess your current level of faith and ask God to increase it over the next year.

_____ **The Power of 1°**

Genesis 22:6-13

6 And Abraham took the wood of the burnt offering and laid it on Isaac his son. And he took in his hand the fire and the knife. So they went both of them together.

7 And Isaac said to his father Abraham, "My father!" And he said, "Here I am, my son." He said, "Behold, the fire and the wood, but where is the lamb for a burnt offering?"

8 Abraham said, "God will provide for himself the lamb for a burnt offering, my son." So they went both of them together.

9 When they came to the place of which God had told him, Abraham built the altar there and laid the wood in order and bound Isaac his son and laid him on the altar, on top of the wood.

10 Then Abraham reached out his hand and took the knife to slaughter his son.

11 But the angel of the Lord called to him from heaven and said, "Abraham, Abraham!" And he said, "Here I am."

12 He said, "Do not lay your hand on the boy or do anything to him, for now I know that you fear God, seeing you have not withheld your son, your only son, from me."

13 And Abraham lifted up his eyes and looked, and behold, behind him was a ram, caught in a thicket by his horns. And Abraham went and took the ram and offered it up as a burnt offering instead of his son.

Abraham took Isaac and some supplies to the place God commanded them to go. Somewhere along the final stretch of the journey, Isaac asked his father where the lamb was for the burnt offering. When Isaac asked why they didn't have a lamb, Abraham answered that God would provide the lamb. This answer required an incredible amount of faith, as indicated in Hebrews 11:18-19.

Think about it - Abraham, well over 100 years old, bound his son, Isaac, to sacrifice him. Isaac could have easily fled his father or struggled free, but there is no indication he did. In fact, there is every indication that Isaac was completely submissive to everything his father asked of him. There are a lot of similarities between Isaac and Jesus:

- Both were their father's one and only son.
- Both had a three day journey – one to the mountain, one to a tomb.
- Both used a donkey.
- Both were noted as beloved.
- Both births were considered not just unlikely, but impossible.
- Both carried the wood on their shoulders they were to die upon.
- Both of them worshipped and returned to their rightful place.
- Both of them were released from death on the third day.
- Both of them completely submitted to their father in every way.

We worship a God who is faithful - always faithful - without exception. He is completely reliable in delivering on every single promise He has ever made. Every prophecy He has spoken has been fulfilled in its due time and we can be confident He will fulfill all remaining prophecies in the same manner. You and I will never be disappointed with God's consistency.

When we lead people into the presence of God during our worship experiences, do we tap into God and His power? Do we celebrate His consistency? Do we intentionally help others experience the same joy we have because of His faithfulness? Let's recognize the power we have in Christ and share it with others every chance we get.

Question(s) of the Week: *Are you willing to go to the ends of the earth to obey God?*

Worship Leader: *Ask your team: Are there any particular areas in your life where you have become spiritually lazy in obeying God?*

_____ *The Power of 1°*

[Optional Materials: A piece of clay **]**

Jeremiah 18:1-6

1 The word that came to Jeremiah from the Lord:

2 "Arise, and go down to the potter's house, and there I will let you hear my words."

3 So I went down to the potter's house, and there he was working at his wheel.

4 And the vessel he was making of clay was spoiled in the potter's hand, and he reworked it into another vessel, as it seemed good to the potter to do.

5 Then the word of the Lord came to me:

6 "O house of Israel, can I not do with you as this potter has done?" declares the Lord. "Behold, like the clay in the potter's hand, so are you in my hand, O house of Israel."

The Lord had a message for Jeremiah. When Jeremiah arrived at the potter's house, the potter was working the clay. To the potter, the clay appeared spoiled and marred. There was a flaw in its design. There were imperfect formations and impurities in its structure. The potter was not pleased with its existing form.

Did the clay have any say in the matter? Could the clay tell the potter that he liked things just the way they were? Did the potter have any inclination to allow the clay to have input into the final product? No. The ultimate product was in the vision and hands of the potter. The clay was simply to accept what the potter desired to do with it. So the potter reworked the clay into another vessel; one that ultimately seemed good in the potter's eyes.

In this parable, God is the Potter and we are the clay. He has a vision for the type of vessel He wants each of us to become. Some of us may be like the ordinary clay pot and carry water. Others of us may be more ornate in personality and design. Still others may be creativity crafted for unique purposes while all of us have a specific reason for how we have been crafted by God. Only the Potter knows what type of vessel He wants each of us to become. It is our privilege as believers and worshippers to listen and discover what His plans are for our lives.

Worshipper, are you allowing the molding and glazing process of the Potter to take effect in your life? Are you setting aside your own personal desires and listening to the leading of the Holy Spirit? Or do you run from any type of spiritually painful process that may assist you in becoming all that the Potter desires for you? Intense pressure and heat is required at times to change us from who we are today into what the Potter wants us to become. Look intentionally at your life and evaluate whether you have given God, the Potter, the ability to do whatever He wants with you.

Question(s) of the Week: What areas are you resistant to the Potter molding you into what He wants you to become?

Worship Leader: Encourage your team: Tenaciously pursue God and what He has created you to become.

_____ **The Power of 1º**

Equal Judgment

Matthew 7:1-5

1 *"Judge not, that you be not judged.*

2 *For with the judgment you pronounce you will be judged, and with the measure you use it will be measured to you.*

3 *Why do you see the speck that is in your brother's eye, but do not notice the log that is in your own eye?*

4 *Or how can you say to your brother, 'Let me take the speck out of your eye,' when there is the log in your own eye?*

5 *You hypocrite, first take the log out of your own eye, and then you will see clearly to take the speck out of your brother's eye."*

These verses tell us a lot about how judging other Christians actually affects us more than them. As seen here, we are judged with the same measurement stick as the one we use to judge others. We should be more severe in evaluating our own sin compared to that of another believer. The entire plank in our own eye is priority number one. A spiritual self-examination is in order before even considering pointing out another believer's sins and weaknesses. Then and only then can we clearly see with Christ-illuminated eyes to help a Christian brother or sister become aware of their sin.

Sometimes it's easy for us to notice other people's shortcomings isn't it? Our need to feel good about ourselves is enough to drive us to look for these judgmental nuggets to hold onto. At times we may simply harbor judgmental thoughts in our own hearts and minds. We may go a step further and ask a Christian friend to *validate* what we have observed to be true. Going even deeper, we may bring it up as a *prayer request* to make our sin of judging *more spiritual*. Rather than highlight another believer's shortcomings, we should pray for them and work on our own sins.

Do you notice others' shortcomings more than your own? Relating to our worship team, it may start with subtle things: Maybe someone shows up late or doesn't even come to practice. Do you complain about it? You may think another person can put forth more effort than they are. Do you have pride and self-righteousness about your own efforts? Someone else might get privileges you don't. Are you jealous of them? The truth is, we should not judge others, including other worship team members. Be careful to thoroughly assess your own Christian life before approaching your Christian brother or sister about theirs.

If anyone had the right to judge, it was Jesus. He did nothing wrong, yet was spit upon. He never caused His Christian brothers to stumble, but was denied by His closest friends. He didn't deserve to die a cruel death on a cross, but He allowed them to crucify Him anyway. He did all of this because He loved you and me too much not to. Let's follow His example and instructions here and beware of judging others.

Question(s) of the Week: Do you thoroughly examine your own sinful life before judging other Christians?

Worship Leader: Pray now: Ask God to help you and your team members deal with their sins rather than judging others.

The Power of 1°

Proverbs 30:8-9

8 *Remove far from me falsehood and lying; give me neither poverty nor riches; feed me with the food that is needful for me,*

9 *lest I be full and deny you and say, "Who is the Lord?" or lest I be poor and steal and profane the name of my God.*

Luke 11:3

3 *"Give us each day our daily bread"*

Super-Size. *Super* Sonic. *Super* Bowl. *Big* Mac. *Big* Gulp®. *Grand* Piano. *Grand* Canyon. *Grand* Tetons. *Instant* Coffee. *Instant* Messaging. *Supreme* Pizza. *Supreme* Court. *World* Class. *World* Series. *World* Records. Humanity is obsessed with extremes, aren't we? Anything from the biggest to the best, from the fastest to the most extravagant seems to attract our attention. So what does the Bible have to say about how we are to respond to this as His followers?

Solomon recognized the dangers of excessive living (Ecclesiastes 2). He knew there was a fine line between too much and too little. On one hand, if we are given more than we need, the focus of our security turns to the excess in our lives. On the other hand, if we are given less than we need, we have a tendency to become bitter, resentful and possibly take advantage of others to take care of our own needs. Neither extreme is healthy nor Godly.

Here we see an example of a Christian that wants nothing more than to walk in faith with the Lord daily and trust Him for everything. Not just in small, insignificant details of His life, but for life-sustaining provision from the Lord. Our Lord wants us to be dependent on Him alone. Not in ourselves. Not in our possessions or money. Not in anything this world has to offer. Our faith and security should be in our Jehovah Jireh, our Great Provider, and nothing else.

In Solomon's day, bread was made on a daily basis. It was not stored away for the week, but made every single day by hand for that particular day only. If they made too much bread, it would spoil. If they did not make enough bread, people would go hungry. Solomon's desire was to only receive what was necessary for the moment. He wasn't looking for leftovers. He didn't need a savings account. He had no backup plan. His faith and trust was in God alone. As worship leaders and team members, we should follow His lead. Are you living with this kind of faith or are you obsessed with always acquiring more?

Question(s) of the Week: *Are you content in God providing you with "daily bread" or do you have an insatiable appetite for more?*

Worship Leader: *Pray now: Ask God to help your team members recognize that it is God who provides for them and they should be content in Him, not wrapped up in pursuing worldly possessions.*

The Power of 1°

2 Samuel 6:13-15

13 And when those who bore the ark of the Lord had gone six steps, he sacrificed an ox and a fattened animal.

14 And David danced before the Lord with all his might. And David was wearing a linen ephod.

15 So David and all the house of Israel brought up the ark of the Lord with shouting and with the sound of the horn.

David was scared. He had just witnessed Uzzah die because he touched the ark of the Lord to stabilize it when the oxen stumbled. Even though Uzzah probably meant well in catching the ark, he disobeyed God's command to not touch it. Out of fear in proceeding, David stopped at Obed-edom's house. He waited there for three months. During this period, David watched everything in Obed-edom's house be blessed, because the ark of the Lord was with them.

After observing these blessings, David decided to proceed in taking the ark to the city of David. To verify that God's blessing had not left them, David and his men carried the ark six steps. Nothing devastating happened. No one died. God's hand of blessing was still with the ark of the Lord. To celebrate this, David sacrificed an ox and a fattened animal. By doing so, he worshipped the Lord.

Then David did something amazing. He *danced with all his might* in a linen ephod before the Lord in front of everyone nearby. This was considered disgraceful attire and far below the garments of a king. For a king, it was seen as foolish and inappropriate to wear anything less than the royal garments. Regardless, David danced not for others, but for the Lord. He didn't care what others thought of him. He kept his eyes on God and forgot about people's perceptions around him. He humbled himself as king and brought glory to God.

In some churches, there can be unspoken expectations of the way people *should* worship. It may include how much (or how little) people raise their hands. It might be whether or not the congregation primarily observes or participates in worship. Then again, there is always the preference of style, speed, volume, etc. of the songs. God cares much less about these details and looks at the hearts and motivations of those worshipping Him. It is less about *how* we worship and more about *who* we worship. We should maintain a Christ-centered worship experience and avoid simply pleasing others in their personal preferences.

Question(s) of the Week: *When worshipping God, do you worship with all your might, or do you restrain yourself because of church norms and the perceptions of others?*

Worship Leader: *Ask your team: Regarding worship, what unhealthy expectations, spoken or unspoken, does our church currently have and how can we overcome them?*

The Power of 1°

2 Samuel 6:20-22

20 And David returned to bless his household. But Michal the daughter of Saul came out to meet David and said, "How the king of Israel honored himself today, uncovering himself today before the eyes of his servants' female servants, as one of the vulgar fellows shamelessly uncovers himself!"

21 And David said to Michal, "It was before the Lord, who chose me above your father and above all his house, to appoint me as prince over Israel, the people of the Lord - and I will celebrate before the Lord.

22 I will make myself yet more contemptible than this, and I will be abased in your eyes. But by the female servants of whom you have spoken, by them I shall be held in honor."

David just finished celebrating the Lord bringing the ark to its designated place in the tent, within the city. He was so overjoyed to see God blessing the Israelites that he offered up burnt offerings and peace offerings to the Lord. He then blessed men and women alike throughout all of Israel by providing them with food to take home to their families. Not just any food, but a substantial portion; including bread, meat and a cake of raisins.

As David entered the city his wife, Michal, watched from her window as David danced and leaped in the streets. She despised him because of his actions. She was embarrassed to watch her husband, the king, humiliate himself by dancing the way he did for everyone to see. Since he was the king, her expectations were that he would behave like a king: noble, mature, strong, wise and honorable.

When Michal approached David, she was sarcastic and disrespectful, criticizing his behavior. David pointed out to her that God chose him, above her father, to lead Israel. David's response was one of correction and rebuking. He stated he would become even more humiliated and contemptible before the Lord. While David and Michal both witnessed the same expression of David's worship, their interpretation was radically different. How was David's response different than Michal's?

- David worshipped God.
  - **Michal judged David.**

- David was elated towards God.
  - **Michal despised David.**

- David abandoned his nobility, prestige and position to worship the Lord.
  - **Michal showed no regard or recognition of God.**

- David sacrificed to the Lord.
  - **Michal scrutinized David.**

- David blessed the Lord with his actions.
  - **Michal saw only how other people would perceive David.**

- David tried to please God and ignore people's perspectives.
  - **Michal tried to please people and ignore God's perspective.**

Question(s) of the Week: Do you focus more on pleasing God or pleasing people? In what specific ways?

Worship Leader: Ask your team: Think for a moment... who do you try to impress other than God? Your spouse? Leaders? Others?

The Power of 1°

2 Samuel 7:7

7 'In all places where I have moved with all the people of Israel, did I speak a word with any of the judges of Israel, whom I commanded to shepherd my people Israel, saying, "Why have you not built me a house of cedar?"'

David took a step back from everything going on to view his situation. He saw his own beautiful palace made of cedar while the ark was residing in a simple tent. This disturbed David. He felt it was only reasonable for the ark to be in a more prestigious place. So he consulted the prophet Nathan. Nathan thought it was a noble idea and told David that God was with him. There was only one problem: neither David nor Nathan consulted God on the idea of building a new residence for the ark.

That same night, God told Nathan to ask David two questions. First, he was to ask David if God told him to build a temple for the ark. Second, he was to ask David if God had ever told any leader to build a temple for the ark. Both of these questions resulted in the resounding answer, "no". While God may have been pleased with David's intentions, it was not God's will for David to build the temple (1 Kings 8:18-19).

David and Nathan made what seemed to be good, God-honoring plans, but did not get God's perspective, guidance or approval. They weren't intentionally disobeying God, but equally as bad, they weren't seeking His will. They made decisions that seemed Godly from a human perspective, but not what God desired for them.

Worshippers, sometimes we can fall into the same trap, can't we? We start heading down a path we believe is God-honoring, just to spiritually wake up and realize we have not sought the Lord's guidance and direction. We then recognize that the path we have chosen has led us away from where God really wanted us to be.

It takes discipline and patience to listen to what God wants for our lives. Before choosing what to do for the Lord, seek the Lord Himself. Then ask Him what His desire is for you regarding your work, family and ministry. In the end, we are at our best when we follow His lead, because our Father knows best.

Question(s) of the Week: *What decision(s) have you made recently that you have not sought God's direction on yet? How are you going to address this?*

Worship Leader: *Challenge your team: Please be praying for us as church leadership that we will clearly hear God's voice and obey Him.*

The Power of 1°

Ephesians 6:1

1 Children, obey your parents in the Lord, for this is right.

John 10:10b

10b "I came that they may have life and have it abundantly."

Children, obey your parents. We may have heard this verse many times, but how often do children not listen to their parents? As Godly parents we love our children and desire the best for them. We long to help guide them in making good decisions. We want them to achieve their greatest potential and be successful in life. We don't want to make their lives miserable - we want them to enjoy life to the fullest. And just because we say *no* at times doesn't mean we want to hold them back in life, right? So, why don't they seem to understand all this?

As worship leaders and team members, we have some of these same childish tendencies, don't we? We want to make *our* own decisions. We want *our* musical preferences. We don't want to listen to advice that goes against *our* own desires. We tell God what *we* want and expect to get it. Too often *we* look to God to answer *our* prayers the way *we* think they should be answered rather than allowing Him to answer how He desires.

The truth is this: Our Father passionately loves us and fervently pursues us. He wants the best for us. He deeply desires that we draw close to Him and put our full faith in Him. Not partial or selective faith – but our full faith. In fact, as the scripture states, He wants us to have life and have it to the fullest. This is a God that loves us intimately as His children!

Scripture tells us that Christ followers will hear God's voice. But many times *life* gets in the way and we become disconnected from Him. We need to learn to be quiet and listen to God. We shouldn't come and tell Him *our personal agenda*. Like sheep to the Good Shepherd, we should hear His voice and follow Him. As we mature in our faith, we will recognize that God's desires and plans are always best. Not sometimes. Not most of the time. All of the time. We need to be still and be quiet. We should maintain a posture of listening more and speaking less. As we worship Him, He has a message for us and the only way we can follow Him is to be alert, listen and obey. Ultimately, we need to become *master listeners* by listening to the Master.

Question(s) of the Week: *Where are you acting on your own accord and not listening to the Master's directions?*

Worship Leader: *Challenge your team: Pray this week and listen to God without having any requests or an agenda. See what He says.*

——————————————————————— *The Power of 1°*

Luke 15 (Portions)

11 And he said, "There was a man who had two sons.

12 And the younger of them said to his father, 'Father, give me the share of property that is coming to me.' And he divided his property between them.

13 Not many days later, the younger son gathered all he had and took a journey into a far country, and there he squandered his property in reckless living.

14 And when he had spent everything, a severe famine arose in that country, and he began to be in need.

20 And he arose and came to his father. But while he was still a long way off, his father saw him and felt compassion, and ran and embraced him and kissed him.

21 And the son said to him, 'Father, I have sinned against heaven and before you. I am no longer worthy to be called your son.'

28 But he [the older brother] was angry and refused to go in. His father came out and entreated him,

29 but he answered his father, 'Look, these many years I have served you, and I never disobeyed your command, yet you never gave me a young goat, that I might celebrate with my friends.

30 But when this son of yours came, who has devoured your property with prostitutes, you killed the fattened calf for him!'

31 *And he said to him, 'Son, you are always with me, and all that is mine is yours.*

32 *It was fitting to celebrate and be glad, for this your brother was dead, and is alive; he was lost, and is found.'"*

In this story, the younger brother wanted to receive his inheritance and leave home. So he did just that - he left home and squandered all his money on wild living. A famine hit across the land and he was ultimately hired to feed pigs. After reaching exhaustion and coming to his senses, he recognized his poor choices. He returned home, hoping to be a common servant for his father. As he approached his home though, his father ran to him from a distance and embraced him. His father then held a party celebrating his youngest son's return.

Meanwhile, the older son that stayed home heard the sounds of the party as he came near the house. When he inquired about it, a servant told him his younger brother had returned home and their father was throwing a party for him. The older brother was furious and refused to join the party. Eventually, the father went out to ask him to join the celebration over his younger brother coming home.

This story is commonly known as *The Prodigal Son*. But which son ultimately pleased God? Was it the younger son that left home and squandered his wealth? In the end, he returned home repentant and humbly prepared to serve his father. His father celebrated his return and raised him to his rightful place. Or was it the less popular, older son that stayed home? He obeyed his father through his actions but his attitude was altogether different. In the end, he became a prideful, judgmental individual that was obsessed with his own goodness.

As worshippers and worship leaders, we can become preoccupied with our own human goodness while overlooking our pride, arrogance and sin. We tend to see the good in ourselves but the shortcomings of others. This artificially inflated perspective gives us a skewed sense of reality. It is time for each of us to accept reality for what it is. We need to ask God to reveal the hidden places in our lives where we are deceived in our perception of ourselves and others.

Question(s) of the Week: *Where are you inflating your perception of yourself while deflating your perception of others? What steps will you take to more accurately see yourself and others from God's perspective?*

Worship Leader: *Pray now: Ask God to reveal where your perceptions are not reality and how He wants you to view yourself and others.*

--- *The Power of 1°*

Know Nothing but Christ

1 Corinthians 2:2

2 *For I decided to know nothing among you except Jesus Christ and him crucified.*

John 17:3

3 *"And this is eternal life, that they know you the only true God, and Jesus Christ whom you have sent."*

Paul was known for putting first things first. He was intentional and determined to remain focused on doing only what was in God's will. Here Paul addresses an essential practice of the Christian faith. He makes the declaration that above all else, he desires to know Jesus Christ and Him crucified.

Before we came to know God, the object of our worship was ourselves. This is human nature. We thought about *our* desires, we set *our* goals and we pursued *our* dreams. Then something significant happened. Through the prompting and leading of the Holy Spirit our lives changed forever. We came to know God, or rather became known by God, through the blood of Jesus Christ.

As musicians, we can get so wrapped up in the musical elements of worship that we forget why we do what we do each week. Worship songs are great, but they should not be the focus of our worship. Sure, bringing our best musical skills and abilities is important to a healthy worship ministry, but isn't there more? Is there a difference between what we do in leading people in worship each week and a group of secular musicians outside of the church? There is a difference, isn't there? The answer is this: The *object of our worship*, Jesus Christ Himself, *is* the difference.

We need to know Jesus deeply and personally. It's not enough to just know about Him or even to know scripture. We need to know the person and character of Jesus Christ. The depths to which we know Him directly impact the depths in which we worship Him. If we know Him in a shallow way, our worship will be shallow. If we know Him deeply, our worship will be deep.

We should each put forth much more effort in getting to know the *object* of our worship, *Jesus*, rather than the *method* of our worship, *music*. Do you want to be a better worshipper? Get to know Jesus Christ, the One you worship, better! The bottom line is this: you can only worship God as deeply as you know Him.

Question(s) of the Week: With Jesus Christ being the "object" of your worship, what has hindered your efforts to get to know Him better?

Worship Leader: Ask your team: Ask someone to pray God will give you and your team a renewed passion to know Christ in a deeper way.

The Power of 1°

Matthew 5:41

41 *"And if anyone forces you to go one mile, go with him two miles."*

"Have it Your Way". "You Deserve a Break Today". "It's All About You". "Because You're Worth It". "Just Do It." We hear phrases like these all the time from marketing ads. We are told that we have *earned this* and *deserve that* and if we don't act upon our own selfish desires immediately, somehow we are missing out. But Jesus spoke against this mindset.

In Jesus' day, a Roman mile was 1,000 paces, or about 142 yards shy of what we know today as our English mile. The king's messengers were permitted and even empowered to commandeer horses, chariots and common men. Regardless of what these other men were involved in at the time, the king's messenger could compel or force the individual to assist him on his journey for one Roman mile. These common people were told to leave their work, families and lives to help a complete stranger and refusing to help was not an option. This was many times inconvenient at best and intrusive at worst.

Jesus is giving us a life lesson here. He is telling us to not only look for ways to help others, but to go the extra mile in the process. People all around us need help. Worship team members, church members, co-workers, friends and family – even those we don't get along with or agree with. It is up to us to remain close to our Heavenly Father to discern when and where He is calling us to be His hands and feet.

Thinking through your circle of influence, is there anyone close to you that needs you to *go the extra mile with them* through this time in their life? Anyone within our church or worship ministry? Any friends or family members? Once God reveals someone to you, go the extra mile for them. Show them an abundance of God's love and character. Care for them excessively. Encourage them extravagantly. Love them lavishly. Support them sacrificially. Carry their burdens courageously. Show them Christ in an extraordinary way. Jesus did this for us. Let's go and do likewise for others.

Question(s) of the Week: *Who is God bringing to your mind right now for you to walk the second mile with?*

Worship Leader: *Pray now: Ask God to show you and your team members how He wants you to walk the extra mile with people.*

The Power of 1°

John 15:1-11

1 "I am the true vine, and my Father is the vinedresser.

2 Every branch in me that does not bear fruit he takes away, and every branch that does bear fruit he prunes, that it may bear more fruit.

3 Already you are clean because of the word that I have spoken to you.

4 Abide in me, and I in you. As the branch cannot bear fruit by itself, unless it abides in the vine, neither can you, unless you abide in me.

5 I am the vine; you are the branches. Whoever abides in me and I in him, he it is that bears much fruit, for apart from me you can do nothing.

6 If anyone does not abide in me he is thrown away like a branch and withers; and the branches are gathered, thrown into the fire, and burned.

7 If you abide in me, and my words abide in you, ask whatever you wish, and it will be done for you.

8 By this my Father is glorified, that you bear much fruit and so prove to be my disciples.

9 As the Father has loved me, so have I loved you. Abide in my love.

10 If you keep my commandments, you will abide in my love, just as I have kept my Father's commandments and abide in his love.

11 These things I have spoken to you, that my joy may be in you, and that your joy may be full."

This passage is a metaphor: Jesus is The Vine, God is The Vinedresser and Christians are the branches. Jesus is referring to two types of vines: those that bear fruit and those that do not. The vines that bear fruit are true believers who are abiding in Christ. It is through Christ alone that we have the ability to produce *much fruit*. This includes effectively leading people in worship to God. The branches by themselves cannot bear any fruit at all. As Christians we have absolutely no ability whatsoever of producing spiritual fruit without God moving through us. Only through fellowship and union with Christ can we lead someone into God's presence through worship.

It is by maintaining an active fellowship with the Father that the true believer can produce the fruit God desires to fulfill through them. This requires being quiet, actively listening and responding in obedience. Sometimes hearing God's will is simple and straightforward. Other times it requires patience, tenacity and sheer spiritual grit.

To the branches that do not produce fruit, the Vinedresser (God) cuts off and removes. This shows a stark contrast between authentic Christians and people who profess to be Christians but do not abide in Christ. To the branches that do produce spiritual fruit, God prunes so they can produce even more fruit. This process can be uncomfortable and even painful at times; but in growing to maturity, it is necessary and one the Vinedresser knows is essential for growth.

As worshippers, our goal should be to produce the fruit God wants to create through us, not what we want to produce for Him. This is accomplished through obedience to Him. We should welcome His pruning. We should invite Him to remove the twigs and debris in our lives so we can be more useful to Him. Sure it's painful. Yes it can be uncomfortable at times. But we are the branches and surrendering our lives to Him means we submit to His will and let Him have His way with us. In response to our obedience, He will fill us with joy that is over-flowing.

Question(s) of the Week: What type of fruit are you producing? What is the Vinedresser pruning in your life?

Worship Leader: Pray now: Ask God to prune those areas in your team that do not reflect Him.

——————————————————— *The Power of 1°*

Matthew 6:19-21

19 *"Do not lay up for yourselves treasures on earth, where moth and rust destroy and where thieves break in and steal,*

20 *but lay up for yourselves treasures in heaven, where neither moth nor rust destroys and where thieves do not break in and steal.*

21 *For where your treasure is, there your heart will be also."*

How many of you have ever been to an estate sale? Why do people go to estate sales? Are they looking for a valuable item at an excellent price? Earthly possessions are often sold in estate sales when people pass away. What a person owns for decades as a prized possession is practically given away to a complete stranger in just a matter of days. Every earthly possession is gone. None are taken beyond this life.

Jesus is giving us a stern warning here against spending our lives pursuing earthly rewards. Why? Because they have no value in God's economy compared to eternal rewards. Every earthly item is temporal and vulnerable to being damaged or stolen. No item is invincible. Every human possession is susceptible to becoming useless or being passed on to someone else.

As Christians there are only two treasure chests we can deposit into: a temporal, earthly treasure chest or an eternal, heavenly treasure chest. One can give us an immediate, short-term gratification. The other lasts forever. God does not desire to limit our treasure, but rather, direct which treasure chest we are depositing into. The treasure chest we value most will be the one we primarily deposit into, reflecting where our heart is focused.

If we are not in tune with the Holy Spirit, we can become distracted by the counterfeit treasures of this world. While earthly gains can provide temporal pleasures, they have absolutely no value or worth in God's eternal economy. Think about it – would you rather have a treasure that is disposable or one that lasts forever?

As worship leaders and team members, we should be leading the example in our passion and desire for having an eternal impact. What type of treasure are you building right now? Are you investing your time in things of this world, or beyond this life? Are you pouring into others here within our worship ministry and church? How much time and energy are you investing in your heavenly bank account? Are you sharing with others the good news of Jesus? There are only two treasure chests we can deposit into. We need to be careful to invest in the right one.

Question(s) of the Week: *Which treasure chest are you depositing into the most?*

Worship Leader: *Ask your team: What are some common 'earthly treasure chests' we tend to excessively deposit into?*

——————————————————————————— **The Power of 1°**

It's Time to Speak Up!

Mark 16:15

15 And he said to them, "Go into all the world and proclaim the gospel to the whole creation."

Romans 10:17

17 So faith comes from hearing, and hearing through the word of Christ.

Jesus is commanding His disciples to proclaim the gospel to the world. As worshippers of God, we are His present day disciples. And what is *the world?* It is everyone around us! It is to our neighbors, friends, co-workers, people both domestic and foreign, grocery store clerks, citizens in Zimbabwe, the rich, the homeless, bank tellers, strangers that appear discouraged and anyone else God puts in our lives.

As Christ followers, if we are not praying and looking for opportunities to share our faith with others, we are grossly missing God's intention for our lives. It is imperative that we verbally tell others about Christ because scripture says *faith comes from hearing through the word of Christ.*

When preparing to share the gospel, we should approach it with a Christ-centered response. What's the difference between our *natural* response and God's?

- We say: "People will see Christ through my good works alone."
  - **Jesus says: "Go...proclaim the gospel to the whole creation." Mark 16:15**

- We say: "I don't know what to say."
  - **God says: "Go...I will be with your mouth and teach you what you shall speak." Exodus 4:12**

- We say: "It's not my spiritual gift."
  - **God says: "...Tell of His Salvation... Declare His glory among the nations..." Psalm 96:2-3**

- We say: "What if I offend them?"
  - **God says: "For the word of the cross is folly to those who are perishing, but to us who are being saved it is the power of God." 1 Corinthians 1:18**

Are you using any of these excuses, or others, to not share your faith? God commands all of His disciples to proclaim the gospel - not just preachers or believers with a specific giftedness. This includes worship leaders and team members! Keep your spiritual eyes open for opportunities to verbally share your faith with others and allow Him to speak through you as He opens the doors.

Question(s) of the Week: When is the last time you shared the good news of Christ with someone?

Worship Leader: *Pray now: Ask God to give you and your team a heart for opportunities to share the truth of Jesus with others.*

The Power of 1°

1 Samuel 15:22

22 And Samuel said, "Has the Lord as great delight in burnt offerings and sacrifices, as in obeying the voice of the Lord? Behold, to obey is better than sacrifice, and to listen than the fat of rams."

Samuel was making a comparison for King Saul. Saul was commanded by God to destroy *all* the Amalekites and *all* they owned. To God, all means all and that's all, all means! Regardless of this command, Saul did not fully obey God. Rather than killing all of the Amalekites, King Saul spared King Agag and the Amalekites' best possessions, so he could sacrifice them to God. Samuel was clarifying for Saul that fully obeying God pleases Him more than sacrificing to the Lord as penitence for sin.

Saul didn't listen and follow through with the message God had delivered through Samuel. He was doing what he thought would please God the most rather than obeying what God had already commanded him to do. Saul had his own ideas and preferences and followed them rather than his Lord. How often do we do the same thing? When God directs us in the way we should go, we should obey Him immediately and completely. God knows what pleases Him the most. We aren't to question Him, but to simply obey Him.

Habitually and intentionally sinning with little more than a quick prayer to ask for forgiveness is unacceptable to God. When sin is prevalent, our fellowship with God is hindered and our ability to authentically worship Him is weakened. Sin dulls our spiritual senses and impairs our aptitude to hear God. God desires true repentance, or turning away from our sin, in our pursuit of obeying Him.

Where are you excusing sin in your life and not fully obeying God? Is there a particular sin you regularly commit which you half-heartedly ask forgiveness for without giving it much thought? Do you ever flippantly think *this is my vice* or *this is my struggle*? By doing so, you are not surrendering your sin to Him or believing you cannot overcome it with God's help. Pray that God will give you a renewed determination to obey Him in the specific areas He is now revealing to you.

Question(s) of the Week: *What is God convicting you of right now? How are you going to respond in obedience?*

Worship Leader: *Pray now: Ask God to give your team members the determination to obey God above service and sacrifice to Him.*

The Power of 1°

[**Optional Materials:** A mirror]

John 3 (Portions)

26 *And they came to John and said to him, "Rabbi, he who was with you across the Jordan, to whom you bore witness - look, he is baptizing, and all are going to him."*

28 *You yourselves bear me witness, that I said, 'I am not the Christ, but I have been sent before him.'*

30 *"He must increase, but I must decrease."*

John's followers were disturbed. People that had initially followed John were now following Jesus. This caused John's followers to become concerned and distracted from what they were called to do. But John didn't respond the same as his friends. Not only did John look forward to Jesus coming, he prepared for it and was excited when He arrived!

John clearly understood his place in relationship to Christ. Originally John wanted to attract everyone's attention to himself so he could proclaim the Good News of Jesus and that Jesus would be coming soon. When Jesus arrived on the scene, John's role changed. Now John steps aside and allows Jesus to get the attention. The focus had to shift from John's message of the coming of Jesus to the arrival of Jesus and believing in Him. John was humble enough to fulfill his calling by submitting the attention to Jesus.

John made his life less and less about himself and more about Jesus. We should do the same. As worship leaders and team members, we need to be like a mirror reflecting Christ and nothing else. If we draw attention to ourselves, we become a distraction and a barrier to people during worship. That's exactly what Satan wants. But God desires for us to point people to Him alone.

Whether we play an instrument or sing, we are all working together to lead others in authentic worship to God. Don't be someone's barrier to worship. As you participate in leading, be alert to what you are displaying to others. Be careful to not be a distraction.

Christ must increase and we must decrease. As worshippers we need to get out of the way during worship so He receives *all* the praise. God receives the greatest glory when we draw the least attention to ourselves and the most to Him.

Question(s) of the Week: *Are you drawing attention to yourself rather than God? How can you reflect God more effectively to others?*

Worship Leader: *Lead now: Consider creating a video of each worship service. Watch the video while "muting the* *sound" to identify potential non-verbal elements that may be distracting others from authentic worship.*

The Power of 1°

Scripture References by Week

Week 01 - *Proverbs 4:27*

Week 02 - *Nehemiah 3:1*

Week 03 - *James 4:6*

Week 04 - *Matthew 18:15-17*

Week 05 - *Matthew 5:43-47*

Week 06 - *1 John 2:3*

Week 07 - *Deuteronomy 5:7*

Week 08 - *Genesis 4:1-7*

Week 09 - *Numbers 12:1-10a*

Week 10 - *Ephesians 5:1*

Week 11 - *Matthew 27:50-54*

Week 12 - *Daniel 3 (Portions)*

Week 13 - *Mark 14:26*

Week 14 - *Psalm 100:1*

Week 15 - *Psalms 100:2-5*

Week 16 - *Mark 10:17-22, 1 Samuel 16:7b*

Week 17 - *Exodus 2:11-14, Exodus 3 (Portions)*

Week 18 - *Proverbs 14:30, Ecclesiastes 4:4*

Week 19 - *Psalm 46:10a*

Week 20 - *Colossians 3:23-24*

Week 21 - *Luke 4:14-16, Hebrews 10:24-25*

Week 22 - *Luke 10:38-42*

Week 23 - *Matthew 12:9-14*

Week 24 - *Mark 9:20-24*

Week 25 - *Mark 9:25-29*

Week 26 - *Luke 5:15-16*

Week 27 - *John 2:13-16*

Week 28 - *Matthew 5:5*

Week 29 - *1 Chronicles 16 (Portions)*

Week 30 - *Mark 10:42-45*

Week 31 - *2 Corinthians 10:5b*

Week 32 - *Matthew 16:24*

Week 33 - *Matthew 23:23*

Week 34 - *2 Corinthians 12:7b-10*

Week 35 - *1 Samuel 3:4-10*

Week 36 - *Genesis 22:1-5*

Week 37 - *Genesis 22:6-13*

Week 38 - *Jeremiah 18:1-6*

Week 39 - *Matthew 7:1-5*

Week 40 - *Proverbs 30:8-9, Luke 11:3*

Week 41 - *2 Samuel 6:13-15*

Week 42 - *2 Samuel 6:20-22*

Week 43 - *2 Samuel 7:7*

Week 44 - *Ephesians 6:1, John 10:10b*

Week 45 - *Luke 15 (Portions)*

Week 46 - *1 Corinthians 2:2, John 17:3*

Week 47 - *Matthew 5:41*

Week 48 - *John 15:1-11*

Week 49 - *Matthew 6:19-21*

Week 50 - *Mark 16:15, Romans 10:17*

Week 51 - *1 Samuel 15:22*

Week 52 - *John 3 (Portions)*

Notes

56792023R00083

Made in the USA
Columbia, SC
04 May 2019